Strategic Studies Institute Monograph

RUSSIA AND THE CURRENT STATE OF ARMS CONTROL

Stephen J. Blank
Editor

September 2012

*****

Comments pertaining to this report are invited and should be forwarded to: Director, Strategic Studies Institute, U.S. Army War College, 47 Ashburn Drive, Carlisle, PA 17013-5010.

*****

*****

The Strategic Studies Institute publishes a monthly e-mail newsletter to update the national security community on the research of our analysts, recent and forthcoming publications, and upcoming conferences sponsored by the Institute. Each newsletter also provides a strategic commentary by one of our research analysts. If you are interested in receiving this newsletter, please subscribe on the SSI website at *www.StrategicStudiesInstitute. army.mil/newsletter/*.

ISBN 1-58487-540-2

CONTENTS

FOREWORD

Arms control remains the central issue in U.S.-Russian relations. This is so for many reasons, not least of which are the respective capabilities of these two states and their consequent responsibility for preventing both nuclear proliferation and the outbreak of war between them. Thus the state of the bilateral relationship is usually directly proportional to the likelihood of their finding common ground on arms control. To the extent that they can find such ground, chances for an agreement on what have been the more intractable issues of regional security in Eurasia and the Third World grow, and the converse is equally true.

Because of the centrality of this issue for Russian and U.S. defense and foreign policies, we are pleased to offer this volume, the second in a series of monographs that originated in the third annual conference on Russia held by the Strategic Studies Institute (SSI) at Carlisle Barracks on September 26-27, 2011. The chapters focus on Russian developments in the light of the so-called New Start Treaty that was signed by Russia and the United States in Prague, Czech Republic, in 2010 and ratified by both states later that year. This panel, like the others at the present and previous conferences, allowed experts from the United States, Europe, and Russia to gather together for a candid and spirited discussion of the issues. In this panel, we assembled three well-known U.S. specialists, Former Ambassador Steven Pifer (Ambassador to Ukraine) of the Brookings Institution; Dr. Jacob Kipp, formerly of the Army's Command and Staff College at Fort Leavenworth, KS; and Peter Huessy of the Air Force Association, to discuss these perspectives. As could be expected, their views often diverge, but are also far-ranging and frank, as befits scholarly discussion and expert debate.

SSI is pleased to present this monograph dealing with such a critical issue, and we hope that readers will engage us further in the kinds of issues and debates that surfaced at the conference and that the chapters presented here capture and extend. The overriding importance of nuclear issues for both national and international security mandates our continuing close scrutiny of other nuclear states' outlooks on the entire range of issues associated with nuclear weapons.

DOUGLAS C. LOVELACE, JR.
Director
Strategic Studies Institute

CHAPTER 1

RUSSIA'S FUTURE ARMS CONTROL AGENDA AND POSTURE

Jacob W. Kipp

THE ARMS CONTROL CONTEXT: 2 DECADES OF U.S.-RUSSIAN RELATIONS AFTER THE COLD WAR

Until the end of the Cold War, arms control and disarmament were dominated by the United States and the Soviet Union, with the two superpowers possessing nuclear arsenals of such scale and sophistication as to make their bilateral arrangements the center of gravity of the international system. With the collapse of the Soviet Union, Russia inherited the Soviet part of that arsenal and continued to follow a line of arms control and disarmament as a means to pursue a geostrategic partnership with the United States. In January 1993, Presidents George H. W. Bush and Boris Yeltsin signed the second Strategic Arms Reductions Treaty (START II), which called for a reduction of strategic nuclear arsenals on each side to 3,500 warheads.

Ultimately, Russia's internal crisis and American sentiments of exceptionalism precluded such a partnership. The ratification of START II was delayed, the U.S. Senate did not ratify the Treaty, even with conditions, until 1996, and the Russian Duma did not ratify the agreement until 2000, making that ratification contingent upon the United States upholding the Anti-Ballistic Missile (ABM) Treaty. Washington saw itself as the sole surviving superpower and set itself up as the center of a unipolar world. In this world,

Russia would be treated as just another power with which Washington would deal on a regional basis framed largely by North Atlantic Treaty Organization (NATO) expansion and transformation into an instrument of collective security with the capacity to engage in out-of-area crises. Russia's initial cooperation in such ventures, which included NATO Implementation Forces (IFOR) in Bosnia, came to be seen by Moscow as a mistake when it found itself dealing with instability in its own territory and in the near abroad. At home, the Russian economy declined until 1996, when it began a slow recovery, which was wiped out in the August 1998 collapse of the ruble. Russia appeared to be a marginal international player economically and militarily after the humiliation of its armed forces in Chechnya. Any concern that Washington had about maintaining the appearance of partnership disappeared when it and its NATO allies moved towards overt intervention against Serbia in response to a growing insurgency inside Kosovo and Belgrade's moves to crack down in the province.

Bilateral relations reached a particularly low level when NATO conducted this intervention. When the U.S.-led NATO air campaign did not conclude with Serbian submission after 5 days of bombing, U.S.-Russian relations declined precipitously. When the conflict did end in June 1999, Moscow played a role in brokering the armistice, and its troops, deployed as part of the Stabilization Force (SFOR) in Bosnia, made a symbolic march to Pristina to assert Moscow's status as a player on the ground. That same month, the Russian military conducted its first strategic exercise since the end of the Cold War, Zapad (West) 99, involving simulated nuclear first strikes to counter a NATO intervention against Belarus, which Russian conventional forces could not counter. Late that summer in the face of terrorist actions in Chechnya and elsewhere, Russia intervened to restore Russian sovereignty. At the same time, Vladimir Putin rose rapidly within the Kremlin hierarchy from Chief of the Federal Security Service (FSB), to chair of the Security Council, to Prime Minister, and finally to appointment as President. The Second Chechen War became Putin's war, and it was prosecuted ruthlessly. Putin was elected President of Russia in March 2000. Russian-U.S. relations, which deteriorated during the NATO campaign against Yugoslavia, did not recover during the last years of the Bill Clinton administration. During that period, Putin put Russia on a new path aimed at strengthening state power and bringing about an economic recovery after the decade of crisis associated with the end of the Union of Soviet Socialist Republics (USSR), the attempt to build a market economy, and creation of a democratic polity. Putin proclaimed his goal to be stability and sustained economic development. Democracy would be managed. There was minor progress on some arms control issues late in the Clinton administration. On December 16, 2000, U.S. Secretary of State Madeleine K. Albright and Russian Foreign Minister Igor Ivanov signed the Memorandum of Understanding on Notifications of Missile Launches in the last days of the administration, but progress was not made under the Bush administration, and indeed not until Presidents Barack Obama and Dmitry Medvedev discussed its implementation in June 2010 as part of Obama's Reset policy towards Russia.

A new round of U.S.-Russian relations had to await the outcome of the 2000 U.S. elections, which brought to power George W. Bush. The Bush administration proclaimed the end of the Cold War. Russia did not figure as the chief focus of U.S. foreign policy in the first few months of the Bush administration as it looked to the People's Republic of China (PRC) as an emerging peer competitor. This focus never developed into a sustained policy because of September 11, 2001 (9/11), when U.S. foreign and security policy shifted to the War on Terrorism. Putin's Russia embraced the idea of a common struggle against terrorism and demonstrated a willingness to support strategic arms control if it would provide greater stability and enhance Russia's position as a great power. In December 2001, the Bush administration informed Russia of its intent to withdraw from the ABM Treaty, which the Bush administration described as a relic of the Cold War. Russia's response to the announced U.S. withdrawal was to declare it a "mistake" and to reaffirm the capacity of its strategic nuclear arsenal to remain a viable deterrent force. The State Department under Colin Powell successfully negotiated the Strategic Offensive Reductions Treaty (SORT), which was signed by Presidents Bush and Putin in May 2002. The treaty, which limited strategic offensive nuclear weapons on both sides to 1,700 to 2,200 operationally deployed warheads, was quickly ratified by the U.S. Senate and the Russian Duma in 2003. In the spirit of the post-Cold War era, the treaty did not provide for verification, only bilateral consultations on its implementation. Defenders of withdrawal from the ABM Treaty presented it as a necessary action so that the United States could be free to pursue what the administration described as a limited missile defense capability intended to reduce the risk of attacks from rogue states, who, it was pointed out, were in no way capable of challenging the deterrent capacity of Russia's still extensive strategic nuclear arsenal. In May 2003,

Bush and Putin released a joint declaration aimed at "strengthening confidence and increasing transparency in the area of missile defense." The SORT contained a time limitation of December 31, 2012, when it would expire unless "extended by agreement of the Parties or superseded earlier by a subsequent agreement."

The Treaty survived, but U.S.-Russian relations were particularly rocky during the rest of the Bush administration. Russia had originally supported U.S. intervention in Afghanistan, but when it appeared that intervention would lead to the long-term deployment of U.S. forces, Russia and its partners in the Shanghai Cooperation Organization (SCO), formed in 1996 as the Shanghai Five and becoming the SCO in 2001 with the admission of Uzbekistan, began to express their concerns over such a long-term presence. Russia expressed its hostility toward the U.S. intervention in Iraq, which Moscow saw as an exercise in American unilateral power. Russia expressed its objections to the further expansion of NATO to the east and saw various "color revolutions" in Ukraine, Georgia, and Uzbekistan as subversive attempts to destabilize states within the Russian sphere of influence. NATO discussions of the admission of Ukraine and Georgia to the Alliance brought strenuous objections from Russia. Russia began to pursue arrangements with regimes that had poor relations with Washington, including Venezuela, Syria, and Libya. The U.S. plans for the deployment of radars and interceptor missiles in the Czech Republic and Poland brought another round of debates in Russia over the stability of its deterrent forces and calls for the deployment of short-range, dual-capable Iskander Missile systems to Kaliningrad Oblast'. In August 2008, U.S.-Russian relations reached a particular low when fighting erupted between putative

Russian peacekeepers and Georgian Army units in South Ossetia. The direct intervention of the Russian armed forces brought a quick and decisive end to the fighting, with Russian forces occupying Georgian territory outside of Abkhazia and South Ossetia. Russia in its turn recognized the independence of these two regions from Georgia and stationed military forces on their territory. Prospects for the development of U.S.-Russian relations would depend on the outcome of the U.S. Presidential elections in 2008, although they hardly seemed a major topic in an election dominated by concerns over two ongoing wars and a major financial crisis that was just breaking. The larger question of the U.S. role in the international system did engage both candidates, but the end of a unipolar Pax American, the subtext, was hardly recognized.

THE RESET AND U.S.-RUSSIAN RELATIONS: START III AND GLOBAL ZERO

In keeping with tradition, we found ourselves once again assembled at this august institution, the U.S. Army War College, examining the status of U.S.-Russian relations in anticipation of presidential elections in both states. Four years earlier I suggested there were good prospects for a strategic arms control agreement.[1] Indeed, such an agreement was negotiated by the Obama and Medvedev administrations in 2009 and signed in 2010. This event took place in spite of a major U.S.-Russian confrontation as a result of the August 2008 Russo-Georgian War over South Ossetia and Abkhazia. The Obama administration adopted a policy of "Reset" in U.S.-Russian relations, and much ink was spilled over whether the Reset was real or just for show. Judged by the agreement on strategic offensive arms, the Reset was real. But a bilateral strategic offensive arms control agreement proved far easier to achieve than other parts of the arms control agenda. In part, this was because the Treaty between the United States of America and the Russian Federation on Measures for the Further Reduction and Limitation of Strategic Offensive Arms (START III) addressed well-covered ground from past arms control efforts and reflected a desire by both sides to reduce their strategic nuclear arsenals. This singular achievement, however, was taken to mean different things in Washington and Moscow. This divergence of interpretations is one manifestation of very different views of the international security system and of each power's understanding of its national interests.

From the very beginning of the negotiations, there were very different expectations as to where these negotiations would lead. There were signals from the Obama administration that it was willing to look more pragmatically at U.S.-Russian relations. Missile defense in Europe, which had become a major sore point in relations between Moscow and Washington, was open to reconsideration. In a confidential letter to Medvedev, President Obama had signaled that the United States was willing to give up the interceptor system, which the Bush administration had pushed to deploy in Eastern Europe, in exchange for Russian assistance in limiting arms shipments to Iran, the state whose nuclear ambitions had served to justify the original deployment concept. Washington spoke of deploying other assets and said that it would be willing to consider Russian cooperation in a European missile defense system.[2] Washington signaled a new era of pragmatism in bilateral U.S.-Russian relations, and Moscow greeted the Reset in relations as promising but not proven. For Moscow, the most important product of Reset would be the confirmation of Russia's status as a great power in Eurasia. For the Obama administration, initial pragmatism was a necessary first step to a much more ambitious set of multilateral objectives, of which strategic nuclear weapons reduction was only a part.

On the eve of the meeting of Presidents Obama and Medvedev in London, England, on April 1, 2009, there was significant pressure to tie the bilateral strategic nuclear negotiations to a larger, more ambitious nuclear arms control agenda associated with the Global Zero movement, which had emerged as an international lobby composed of political, military, business, faith, and civic leaders in late 2008. That group mounted an international campaign for the elimination of all nuclear weapons as the best means to end nuclear proliferation, reduce the threat of nuclear terrorism, and eliminate the prospect of nuclear war.[3] Russian commentators noted that the Global Zero movement intended to challenge both presidents to embrace the abolition of nuclear weapons as the most effective means to reduce nuclear proliferation and the threat of nuclear terrorism.[4] Obama and Medvedev did agree to begin negotiations of a new strategic arms control treaty that would cut each nation's long-range nuclear arsenal further than previous agreements. Both Presidents promised a new era in their bilateral relations based upon a more pragmatic relationship.[5]

President Obama used his speech to the Czech people in Prague on April 5, 2009, to declare a U.S. commitment to total nuclear disarmament in the 21st century:

So today, I state clearly and with conviction America's commitment to seek the peace and security of a world without nuclear weapons. (Applause.) I'm not naive. This goal will not be reached quickly—perhaps not in my lifetime. It will take patience and persistence. But now we, too, must ignore the voices who tell us that the world cannot change. We have to insist, "Yes, we can."[6]

By boldly embracing Global Zero, the President set out a longer strategy of great complexity requiring cooperation with a broad range of powers, including Russia. The International Global Zero movement was launched only a few months before the Prague speech by over 300 political, military, business, faith, and civic leaders in December 2008 to mobilize mass opinion to support a phased and verified elimination of all nuclear weapons worldwide. It held out the prospect of Global Zero as a way "to eliminate the nuclear threat—including proliferation and nuclear terrorism—to stop the spread of nuclear weapons, secure all nuclear materials, and eliminate all nuclear weapons: global zero."[7] Given the problems afflicting the remaining Russian nuclear arsenal, Moscow was expected to share Washington's long-range goal. The Russian response to Global Zero, however, reflected a very different military-technical and political appreciation of Global Zero. The devil was in the details, and the first detail was the ratification of START III by the U.S. Senate. Short of the ratification, Moscow simply did not want to talk about other arms control issues.

By June 2009, the divergence of Russian views on Global Zero had emerged with some clarity. Sergei Karaganov, the head of the Council on Defense and Foreign Policy, organized a conference on the issue and invited leading specialists to speak at the conference, which was held at the Higher School of Economics, on "nuclear disarmament and U.S.-Russian relations." Global Zero provided the context for the discussion of one of the most complex aspects of the international system, embracing the security regime, the nature of the international system, the diversity of interests among nuclear powers, and the economic ramifications of general nuclear disarmament. Some analysts, like Aleksei Arbatov, treated the global initiative as the logical extension of bilateral nuclear arms control and a means to ensure the uninterrupted nature of the process of continuing bilateral cooperation in the sphere of nuclear weapon reduction and limitation.

Karaganov, one the most prominent Russian commentators on international security, warned against giving up the deterrent role of nuclear weapons, saying "the world with nuclear weapons is better than the one without them or with them kept at the minimum."[8] He described nuclear weapons as a restraint during the Cold War and noted that the nuclear club's growth was precisely congruent with the post-Cold War period. Noble sentiments and the Non-Proliferation Treaty had not prevented this. Indeed, the two major nuclear powers reduced their arsenals to minimal levels that would increase incentives for third states to acquire a credible deterrent force. Moreover, the absence of nuclear weapons or their reduction to minimal levels could create an incentive for more risky behavior by states, especially the United States, when such adventures carried no risk of strategic retaliation. Karaganov concluded that it would be more useful to pursue a comprehensive bilateral agenda, not tied to Global Zero, to improve U.S.-Russian relations.[9]

Nikolai Spassky, Assistant Director of Rosatom, outlined the many difficulties that would be involved in general nuclear disarmament but warned that Russia had no alternative but to pursue such reductions because progress in military technology would make current arsenals obsolete. This was, so he argued, owing to the fact that "the United States needed but 15 years or so to advance military technologies to the level where availability of nuclear arsenals to its opponents or lack thereof would stop being a factor of deterrence."[10] Other commentators took up this issue, pointing to the abolition of nuclear weapons as robbing Russia of its position as a great power and thus rendering it essentially helpless—first and foremost due to its technological backwardness and slow development."[11]

When the Global Zero movement had its second international summit in Paris, France, in February 2010, both President Obama and President Medvedev expressed support for the general goal of eliminating nuclear weapons. Obama's text spoke of Global Zero as one of his administration's highest priorities. Noting the progress made on the negotiation of a new Strategic Arms Reduction treaty (START) agreement, he laid out a major agenda for the upcoming Nuclear Security Summit in April:

> We will rally nations behind the goal of securing the world's vulnerable nuclear materials in 4 years. We will strengthen the Nuclear Nonproliferation Treaty and work with allies and partners to ensure that the rights and responsibilities of every nation are enforced. We will seek to ratify the Comprehensive Test Ban Treaty and negotiate a Fissile Material Cutoff Treaty. And our Nuclear Posture Review will reduce the role and number of nuclear weapons in our national security strategy.[12]

The focus was on the upcoming Washington Summit and the multinational character of progress towards Global Zero. At the same time, the President said that such progress would not be easy and that the ultimate goal might not be achieved "in our life time."

President Medvedev emphasized the diplomatic context of the meeting, the new content of bilateral U.S. and Russian relations, which included the end of the Cold War, and "an atmosphere of trust and partnership in the relations between leading world powers." Medvedev stressed Russia's commitment to the Treaty on the Nonproliferation of Nuclear Weapons but stressed a contractual path to nuclear disarmament and identified the Russian objective in such negotiations as "a comprehensive long-term strategy of balanced and stage-by-stage reduction of nuclear arsenals under conditions of equal security for all."[13] Nothing would be accepted that endangered the security of Russia. Equal security was not confined to just abolishing nuclear arsenals. Russia required a new security regime which would embrace all of Eurasia.

Progress in the negotiation of START III was significant. Within a year of the meeting of Presidents Obama and Medvedev in London, the negotiators on both sides had a draft treaty ready for the heads of state, and in April 2010 the heads of state met in Prague to sign the treaty, which fostered the impression that the Treaty was a harbinger of what Obama had promised in Prague the year before. The terms of the treaty provided for reduction of each power's number of strategic nuclear missile launchers by half. The treaty limits each side's number of deployed strategic nuclear warheads to 1,550 deployed on bomber aircraft, land-based missiles, and submarine-launched missiles. The cuts were significant when compared with the levels of the original START Treaty of 1991 and the 2002 Moscow Treaty. The treaty also provided for verification by national technical means and by 18 on-site inspections per year.[14] The details appeared in sharp relief during the ratification process in Washington and Moscow.

START'S PROGRESS AND THE ISSUE OF RUSSIAN MILITARY DOCTRINE

As the U.S.-Russian negotiations on START III moved forward, Moscow was also deeply involved in the articulation of a new military doctrine and a nuclear policy document. By the end of 2009, it was clear from the Russian news media that President Medvedev was deeply involved in both processes. The press was full of leaks from leading officials in the Security Council that the military doctrine would contain a statement on first or preemptive use of nuclear weapons. In the immediate aftermath of the signature of Russia's new military doctrine by President Medvedev, most attention focused on the fact that a first nuclear strike was not mentioned in the document and on the charge that NATO was the chief source of "dangers" to the security of the Russian Federation. Comments by NATO's leadership that the doctrine was not a realistic portrayal of NATO were reported by the press, but there was no strong criticism of that aspect of the doctrine. Instead, Russian authors drew attention to the problem of the gap between Russia's conventional military capabilities vis-à-vis NATO and its consequent reliance on nuclear weapons in a conventional conflict. On the day that President Medvedev signed the new military doctrine, Oleg Nikiforov, however, addressed the issue of NATO-Russian relations and explored Western assessments of Russia's military power in a review of a recent article titled "Russian's Military Capabilities: Great Power Ambitions and Reality," by Margarete Klein for the German publication, *Stiftung Wissenschaft und Politik*. In that article, Klein came to the conclusion that Russia's great power pretensions were not based on real military capabilities, and that economic and demographic problems made it unlikely that Russia would achieve such military modernization. Nikiforov noted the prominent place of *Stiftung Wissenschaft und Politik* among German think tanks and its close relationship to Chancellor Angela Merkel's government.

For Nikiforov, the article asked the question whether Russia was a "paper tiger or a real threat" and answered the question with a qualified "both." Russia's military modernization will not create a direct threat to NATO members, but increased capabilities will permit it to intervene more effectively on its periphery, where it will be a real threat to successor states and to the possibility of NATO intervention on the periphery. In this regard, the Russian-Georgian conflict of 2008 appeared to signal the willingness of the Russian government to act even at the risk of creating an international crisis. He also called attention to Klein's negative prognosis on the likelihood of success for the "New Look" of the Russian armed forces, based upon the inability of the arms industry to produce modern weapons in a timely fashion, which leaves the prospect of conflict high and the ability to manage it at the conventional level low. In this regard, Klein recommended a revival of conventional arms control talks in order to reduce the risks of escalation in such conflicts. Nikiforov concluded that under the present circumstances, the West still considers Russia to be a "paper tiger."[15]

An article appearing after the publication of the military doctrine explored the same theme in relation to the doctrine's content. Writing for *Moskovskii Komsomolets*, Olga Bozheva noted that the doctrine appeared on the eve of the Munich Conference on Global and European Security and created quite a stir. There, Russia had raised concerns about the U.S. plan to deploy elements of an ABM system in Rumania, while the West expressed concern about the role of nuclear weapons in Russia's military doctrine. Citing reduced capabilities of early warning in case of nuclear attack and declining offensive nuclear capabilities, Bozheva depicted the doctrine's nuclear pronouncements as a de facto admission of Russia's military weakness. The doctrine, in her view, offers nothing but fine words about the New Look of the armed forces promised by Minister of Defense Serdiukov, and Western leaders are likely to read the Russian defense posture as nothing more than a bluff seeking to conceal real weakness.[16] The bluff will not work for long. At the same time, the new doctrine proclaimed NATO expansion to be the primary danger to Russian security, and the President approved the decision to purchase one of the helicopter amphibious assault ships of the *Mistral* class from France. This contradiction revealed the deeper problem of Russian defense, the absence of a "machine-building complex" to support domestic military requirements. Bozheva labeled the new military doctrine an "anti-military doctrine"[17]

A day before publication of the new military doctrine, Aleksandr Khramchikhin, Deputy Director of the Institute for Political and Military Analysis, drew attention to a potential conflict on the border of Russia which had nothing to do with NATO, but was likely, if unleashed, to lead to a much wider war. Khramchikhin pointed to increased tensions between the Republic of Korea and the Democratic People's Republic of Korea. While noting that such tensions have been a common feature of relations between the two states since the 1953 armistice ending the first Korean War, he sees the present tensions as reflecting the breakdown of the Six Power Talks on the elimination of North Korea's nuclear arsenal and signs of increasing tensions between Beijing and Washington. Khramchikhin declared that neither Seoul nor Pyongyang, and neither Beijing nor Washington, wanted to start a fight, but the large arsenals and the higher tensions could lead to uncontrolled escalation bringing in other powers.

Khramchikhin, who has written extensively over the last few years on China's emergence as a regional superpower and modern military power, notes a basic asymmetry between the armed forces of the North and South Koreas, with the South enjoying technological superiority, but the North prepared to conduct a dogged defense using terrain, engineering obstacles, and tunneling to prevent an early and easy victory. U.S. intervention on the side of South Korea would not fundamentally change that military balance, and would not bring the war to a rapid conclusion. U.S. forces currently are overcommitted in other combat theaters and lack the strategic reserve to occupy the North. In any territory of the North occupied by South Korean and U.S. forces, a partisan movement would emerge to continue the fight. Khramchikhin characterized such a conflict as a catastrophe for everyone, including Russia, except China. Moreover, North Korea could make use of its nuclear arms delivered by short-range missiles and aircraft or as nuclear mines. Such an escalation would demand that China act.

Khramchikhin sees Beijing as moving units into North Korea to occupy those areas still under North

Korean control and backing those elements of the North Korean elite willing to greet Chinese People's Liberation Army (PLA) occupation as a national salvation, with Beijing demanding restoration of the border on the 38th parallel. Khramchikhin foresees this conflict leading to the end of the North Korean regime, huge losses for the Republic of Korea, and serious costs in blood, treasure, and prestige for the United States. "Only China has any prospect of coming out of this war as a victor, but even for it, it would be a very risky and costly game." Khramchikhin makes no mention of the consequences for Russia of such a conflict, even though it borders both North Korean and the PRC.[18]

Just a week after Khramchikhin's article appeared, a group of "NATO Elders" charged with developing NATO's new strategic concept visited Moscow. The group, headed by former U.S. Secretary of State Madeleine Albright, stated that they were there to listen. In addition to meeting with Foreign Minister Sergei Lavrov, Albright also spoke at the Moscow State Institute of International Relations and Institute of International Relations and World Economy. The elders did not address the proposal by President Medvedev for a new treaty on European security, but they did show considerable interest in Russia's new military doctrine and took repeated opportunities to remind Russian audiences of the challenge that China posed for international stability. The elders pointed out that the new Russian military doctrine did not even mention China, while naming NATO's expansion into post-Soviet space as the primary danger for Russian security interests. Andrei Terekhov, citing Russian specialists, explained these remarks as being a result of the increased tensions between Washington and

Beijing after the U.S. announcement of the sale of F-16s to Taiwan, and characterized the new relationship as a "cold war."[19]

The official silence about China's rise and its implications for Russian national interests has been deafening. Sino-Russian cooperation to counterbalance a U.S.-dominated unipolar order made some strategic sense when direct tensions between the United States and China did not seem to carry a risk of conflict. However, Russian observers now see the new tensions as amounting to a "duel" between China and the United States for leadership. So far, there was no great risk that the two powers would come to blows, but it was clear that the two sides were heading towards chilly relations, with Beijing responding to the announced F-16 sale by cutting military-to-military contacts and threatening sanctions against the American firms involved in the arms sales to Taiwan. Vladimir Kuzar' saw the present tensions as marking the end of the mutually advantageous economic partnership between Washington and China, characterized by Niall Ferguson as "Chimerica," as Beijing asserts its regional power and seeks its own solutions to such global issues as Iran and North Korea. He concluded his article by warning that the Sino-American duel "can create new and dangerous tension in world politics." But he does not address the implications of those dangers for Russia's own security.[20]

MOSCOW'S PERSPECTIVE ON START III: TACTICAL GAMBLE AND STRATEGIC CONSEQUENCES

After intense negotiations and the interventions of both President Obama and President Medvedev, Moscow and Washington announced in early 2010 that a new treaty limiting strategic offensive weapons would be signed in April in Prague, replacing the START agreement signed in 1991 and which had lapsed in December 2009. President Medvedev expressed his satisfaction with the pace and outcome of the negotiations: "The draft treaty reflects the balance of interests on both sides and . . . though the negotiation process was not always easy, the negotiators' constructive mindset made it possible to achieve a tremendous result in a short time and produce a document ready for signature."[21] In the Presidential statement describing the treaty, the same press release outlined the chief features of the treaty, mentioning the limits in deployed warheads and on deployed and nondeployed launch vehicles—1,550 deployed nuclear warheads; 800 deployed and nondeployed intercontinental ballistic missile (ICBM) launchers, sea-launched ballistic missiles (SLBMs) launchers, and heavy bombers; and a separate limit of 700 deployed ICBMs, deployed SLBMs, and deployed heavy bombers equipped for nuclear armaments.

It then added a statement not found in U.S. official commentary on the Treaty: "The provisions on the interrelation between strategic offensive and strategic defensive arms, as well as on the growing significance of such interrelation in the process of strategic arms reduction, will be set in a legally-binding format." No such statement was contained in the White House's press release on the Treaty, which stated: "The Treaty does not contain any constraints on testing, development, or deployment of current or planned U.S. missile defense programs or current or planned United States long-range conventional strike capabilities."[22] Moscow press accounts speculated on this difference, subjecting it to close examination.

For the last 8 years, the Russian government has made clear its objections to the decision of the Bush administration to withdraw unilaterally from the ABM Treaty of 1972, emphasizing the relationship between strategic offensive and defensive systems. In an interview published 2 days before the official announcement of the agreement, Sergei Rogov pointed to the disagreement between Washington and Moscow over this relationship between strategic offensive and defensive systems and spectulated on whether Washington would accept the inclusion of any such statement in the treaty:

> All previous START documents acknowledged this link but that was a link to the erstwhile ABM Treaty. I do not think it possible to put any parameters of ABM systems into a treaty dealing with strategic offensive arms. All the same, Obama did acknowledge this link in London last April, so that it might be acknowledged in the preamble after all.[23]

Rogov was suggesting that Moscow would be happy with a statement about the relationship without any explicit treaty article defining the technical features of their relations. He did point to Obama's decision to forgo the Bush administration's plans for a limited ABM system in Europe and its replacement with a theater missile defense system designed to deal with intermediate range ballistic missiles (IRBMs) and not strategic ballistic missiles. Rogov did not see such a system as a threat to strategic stability and noted the possibility of U.S.-Russian cooperation in this area. As to the overall role of the new treaty in the diplomatic Reset between Moscow and Washington, Rogov did not see many signs of deep progress. Russia has agreed to a new START because it has to reduce its own strategic nuclear arsenal, and Washington has agreed because the strategic focus of U.S. relations has shifted away from Moscow and toward the Pacific and China. Rogov expected the United States to continue the development of non-nuclear strategic strike systems and the reshaping of its nuclear arsenal toward more flexible forces.

In the wake of the announcement of the agreement, the Russian press focused on the fact that the treaty reduced the strategic offensive nuclear arsenals of the only two powers possessing such capabilities, seeing it as a reaffirmation of Russia's international position as a major power. They praised the verification provisions, which, while being less intrusive and costly than those in the original START agreement, guaranteed transparency, effectiveness, and increased confidence in the process. Finally, the treaty was expected to serve as an example to other nuclear powers and support both the letter and spirit of the Nuclear Non-Proliferation Treaty and serve as a step toward a world without nuclear weapons. The author noted that in the declaration by Foreign Minister Sergei Lavrov, he expected speedy legislative approval of the treaty: "Following the signing, the treaty will be submitted for ratification without delay. As is expected, this will also be done by the American side." The author, however, did not expect the ratification process to be smooth, pointing to the current conflict between the two political parties in the U.S. Senate. He anticipated that Republican opposition would be concerned about the handling of the issue of the mutual relationship between strategic offensive and defensive systems mentioned in Russian official commentaries and the U.S. position that no binding reference to ABM be included in the Treaty. The author expected a political fight on the U.S. side over the content of the Preamble, which will declare such a relationship but provide no binding technical constraints beyond the terms for termination of the treaty by either party.[24] Certainly, the claim by Chief of the Russian General Staff General Nikolai Makarov, that the treaty language reduced mutual concerns and met Russia's national security interests, seemed to suggest a different interpretation as to its political salience and technical ambiguity. "The treaty clearly defines the mechanism for the control of the entire life cycle of nuclear means, and sets the connection between strategic offensive and defensive armaments."[25]

While the Russian press noted the pledges from Senators John Kerry and Richard Lugar, the ranking members of the Senate Committee on Foreign Relations, to begin the ratification process on the treaty immediately following its signing in Prague, the deeper issue remained as to whether Lugar could bring with him sufficient support from other moderate Republicans to ensure a two-thirds vote for ratification. Given the commitment of the Republican Party since Ronald Reagan to strategic defense, they expected the Senate hearings on the treaty to focus on any hidden agendas that would limit U.S. freedom of action in this area. While former diplomats and arms control experts from both Republican and Democratic administrations have endorsed the treaty as a necessary step towards the development of the Reset in U.S.-Russian relations and toward a global regime to remove nuclear weapons, others have questioned the wisdom of both goals. There exists a significant chance that the current bitter partisan conflict in Washington will reduce any prospect of a speedy, bipartisan ratification process. Nikolai Snezhkov called attention to the remarks of Representative Ileana Ros-Lehtinen, the ranking Republican member on the House Committee on Foreign Relations. She cast the issue of ratification in the context of the emerging competition between the United States and China, asking: "Why limit our military potential by a treaty which completely ignores the capability of China, which, if it decided to do it, could rapidly develop its own large nuclear arsenal?" She went on to promise a detailed review of the treaty's provisions and warned that Republicans would "not permit the slightest harm to America's interests in missile defense." Snezhkov concluded that the fate of the treaty was subject to U.S. partisan politics and the emerging nuclear calculus between Beijing and Washington.[26]

Fedor Lukianov, the editor of *Russia in Global Politics*, provides a deeper explanation of what he calls "the last treaty" from the Cold War era. He notes that since the signing of START I, Moscow has sought to continue the arms control focus of U.S.-Russian relations as a way of assuring its own international position in the face of economic realities to reduce its strategic arsenal. The Bush administration, which declared the Cold War over and then withdrew from the ABM Treaty in 2002, saw no reason to continue such a regime because it limited U.S. freedom of action as the sole superpower. The Obama administration on the other hand, in a reassessment of the U.S. global position, has made the Reset of relations with Moscow part of its national security strategy. This Reset is not between geostrategic equals but between a global power and a regional power, where conflicts threatened to undermine the very flexibility that the Bush administration had so treasured. Both sides engaged in serious negotiations and reached compromise solutions.

Lukianov sees the current treaty as part of a larger strategy associated with moving toward a nuclear-free world, pointing towards the advantages the United States would derive from concluding the treaty as it moved into the April Nuclear Summit and the May conference to review the Nuclear Non-Proliferation Treaty. If Russia sees its position as a leading power confirmed by the treaty, the United States sees it as a tool to shift the focus of nuclear arms reductions to a global forum.

Here, however, Lukianov doubts there will be much progress because the driving force shaping the nuclear arsenals of other parties is not the U.S.-Russian strategic balance, but regional conflicts where nuclear weapons permit weaker powers to maintain credible deterrence against opponents with stronger conventional forces, as is the case of Pakistan vis-à-vis India. Long-range ballistic missiles (LRBMs) are not needed for such deterrence, and tactical nuclear disarmament raises the risk of an intense conventional arms race, including one for Russia when it seeks to secure its own territorial integrity in the case of Chinese aggression. In this sense, Lukianov sees the current treaty as the end of one era of arms control and the beginning of a new and more complex process with global ramifications. So far, he does not foresee the emergence of any sort of global security regime that would justify trust in its ability to manage regional conflicts. Short of the emergence of such a mechanism, the treaty will be seen as a tactical political success in Moscow and Washington but not a breakthrough in global security.[27]

Melor Sturua, the U.S. correspondent for *Izvestiia*, focused on the tactical success of the negotiation process and praised Obama and Medvedev for finding the ways and means to reach workable compromises. In the face of each roadblock, the Presidents used personal meetings and phone conversations to find a way around it. Although both had heavy domestic agendas and other foreign policy concerns, they contributed their time and good will to concluding the negotiation process. Among the compromises to which Sturua draws attention are those associated with Obama's admission of the mutual relationship between offensive and defense strategic weapons systems and the problem of a verification regime. Sturua correctly noted that Obama conceded the mutual relationship but did not agree to technical language that would resolve the issue.

On the verification regime, Sturua noted the claim by Russian negotiators that the concessions made by Soviet negotiators in this area in 1991 were both excessive and costly. The result was a compromise in which Americans agreed to accept changes in such areas as the exchange of telemetric data from missile flights. High-level involvement in the negotiation process brought about progress towards an agreement because both Presidents put a priority on success and were willing to engage their opposite number to resolve difficulties. As to the significance of the agreement, Sturua emphasized the very nature of the process as symbolizing the end of one era and the beginning of another. "The new agreement is not perfect but the fruit of compromise. However, its historical and symbolic significance is huge. It puts an end to the epoch of the Cold War of the 20th century and opens a new page in the area of disarmament in the 21st century."[28]

The problem with this tactical focus on the negotiation *process* itself is that it ignores the limited significance of the cuts both sides will make. Polina Khimshiashvili and Natal'ia Kostenko, noting comments by experts on strategic nuclear arms, called the actual reductions of offensive strategic arsenals minimal, involving no limitations on current plans for military modernization.[29] Moreover, even before the treaty was signed in Prague, concerns about the ratification process in Washington were being voiced.

The signing in Prague put an end to U.S.-Russian strategic arms negotiations. It is still unclear whether it will deepen the bilateral Reset in relations or open what the Obama administration seeks to be the first step towards a global nuclear arms reduction regime. Moscow understands that it will not be at the center of this activity but will become another regional player in a complex process. If that process fails, Russia will have much to lose because of the geostrategic dynamic of nuclear proliferation in Eurasia. Both Medvedev and Obama have made a tactical deal to serve each country's national interests and both have much to fear if the treaty is not ratified and does not bring about the desired response by other powers to agree to limits on their arsenals.

In April 2010, Russian Foreign Minister Sergii Lavrov put the recently signed START document in a global security context, which he saw as increasingly dominated by "interdependence and indivisibility." He called attention to the preamble to the treaty which spoke positively of "the historic goal of freeing humanity from the nuclear threat" and repeated President Medvedev's statement to the Global Zero Forum in Paris: "Today our common task consists in undertaking everything to make deadly weapons of mass destruction to become a thing of the past."[30] At the same time, Lavrov depicted a globalized security environment wherein the Cold War instruments for maintaining strategic stability stagnated or corroded. The Treaty held out the promise of a new security environment. START 2010, as Lavrov referred to the agreement, achieved three objectives: "To draw up an agreement that would, firstly, ensure Russia's national security, secondly, make our relations with the U.S. more stable and predictable, and thirdly, strengthen global strategic security."[31] Lavrov focused upon the reaffirmation of international law as applying to all conflicts among nations so as to exclude the use of force or the threat of the use of force. Lavrov pointed to the need for a new security regime, not the abolition of nuclear weapons, as the critical first step towards greater strategic stability. He also called attention to President Medvedev's proposal for a "comprehensive European security treaty" which would provide a security regime for the Euro-Atlantic world extending from Vancouver to Vladivostok.[32]

START 2010 was an important first step in this process. It could not be conceived as the final product. It had to be developed within the broad context of military security issues, including the systemic relations among "strategic nuclear systems, missile defense, and conventionally armed strategic weapons systems," an indirect reference to U.S. programs to develop global immediate-strike conventional systems.[33] The inclusion of such conventional ICBM and SLBM systems before they have become operational was a de facto recognition of their potential impact upon the strategic nuclear equation. The inability of sensors to discriminate between conventional and nuclear armed warheads would be a highly destabilizing development.

Taking into account the shift in the Obama administration's approach to European missile defense, with the abandonment of the Bush's administration's deployment program and substitution of Patriot and Aegis systems, Lavrov embraced the possibility of a multilateral approach involving Russia, the United States, and "other states and international organizations." Lavrov defined the Russian objectives to be the creation of an evolving security system:

> Our goal is to create a multilateral security regime, the so-called antimissile pool. In practical terms it would become a collective system to respond to missile threats by countering missile proliferation, preventing the existing missile challenges from growing into real missile threats, and neutralizing them with priority being given to politico-diplomatic and economic measures of impact.[34]

This effort would have several parallel tracks: "joint assessment of existing and potential challenges," a system of collective monitoring measures permitting "prompt and effective response," and the formulation of "rules of the game" in the sphere of missile defense.[35] He did not speak of a timetable for these measures but clearly saw progress in this area as a high priority for Russian diplomacy, since success would ensure the stability of START 2010 from the Russian perspective.

Finally, Lavrov addressed the issue of tactical/ nonstrategic nuclear weapons, accepting the topic as a logical one following the ratification of the START 2010. But Lavrov did not limit such discussions to bilateral conversations or to Europe. Instead, he proposed the establishment and expansion of nuclear-free zones as one of the most promising ways to move toward Global Zero. He emphasized the cuts made in the Russian tactical/nonstrategic nuclear arsenal since 1991 and pointed out that these cuts had been made on a unilateral basis. "Presently, Russia's non-strategic nuclear capability is not more than 25% of the Soviet capability in 1991."[36] Follow-on progress would depend upon a shift from a balance based on deterrence and fear to one based upon "the power of our trust in one another." This would require "a harmonious combination of cooperation, based on trust, and legal checks and balances, based on the global security matrix." This matrix would not be built on a unipolar or bipolar order but a mulitpolar system, in which Russia would play a key role in Eurasia.

Russian commentators and experts provided intellectual support for Medvedev's position and laid out their case against Global Zero. In July 2010 Karaganov issued an extended critique of Global Zero. However noble the sentiments that stimulated the effort, he labeled its objective as utopian and dangerous. Beginning with a review of trends reshaping the international environment, Karaganov depicted a system that is in flux and inherently unstable. The sources of potential conflict are increasing as the center of the world economy is shifting to the East. At best, nuclear proliferation will be managed and not stopped, and the sources of international conflict are increasing, not diminishing. In this context, Global Zero has no chance of success and can, in fact, increase the risks of conflicts:

> I believe this movement makes no sense. Nobody is going to give up nuclear weapons. Nor is it feasible — technically or politically. One might close the issue by offering a proof of this stance. But I must say that the anti-nuclear movement is harmful. Firstly, it may result in the reduction of nuclear armaments to a dangerous minimum, as it opens the Pandora's Box of negotiations over the reduction of non-strategic nuclear armaments. Secondly, it distracts from the search for

new ways of setting peace and stability in the new world.[37]

Karaganov did not go on to explain what he meant by "opening the Pandora's Box of non-strategic nuclear armaments reductions," but he did point to a conspicuous decline in enthusiasm for Global Zero among the American foreign policy elite, who were now focused on nuclear modernization and remained committed to a system of ballistic missile defense against so-called rogue states. Karaganov described the current environment as one of both "increasing political instability and, worse, a tumult of minds." The increased risks were very close to the instability in the international system prior to World War I and could even be considered "a theoretically pre-war situation," which, however, is still held in check by the existing U.S. and Russian nuclear arsenals.[38]

The existence of the U.S.-Russian nuclear arsenals, when supplemented by the Chinese, French, and British nuclear forces, simply makes general war too risky for any power. Karaganov sees China as a particular beneficiary of this situation since its own nuclear arsenal made impossible a military challenge to China's emerging political-economic power:

> One can hardly conceive China's skyrocketing economic upturn if there had been no Russian-U.S. nuclear parity in the world, which makes any full-blown war inadmissible due to the possibility of its escalation. I will remind that big-time players have been suppressing China's development militarily for about 150 years. At present, this kind of policy appears unthinkable.[39]

Nuclear weapons to Karaganov become that force which Goethe uses to describe Mephistopheles in *Faustus* and which Bulgakov cited at the beginning of *Master and Margarita*: " I am part of that power which eternally wills evil and eternally works good." The immorality of nuclear weapons is unquestioned, but their power imposes restraint upon the actions of princes by holding out the prospect of Armageddon. "They are an effective means of preventing large-scale wars and mass destruction of people — something that humanity has engaged in throughout its history with surprising perseverance, destroying peoples, countries, and cultures."[40]

Humanity has not yet created any other means to prevent such general wars, and so Karaganov sees nuclear weapons as the only existing check on such destruction. "The world has survived only thanks to the nuclear sword of Damocles hanging over it." Karaganov's interpretation of the international system during the Cold War identifies nuclear deterrence as the chief factor that limited conflict and prevented a general war. The nuclear arsenals of the two superpowers had what he calls a "civilizing effect" because it strengthened the hands of pragmatists set on avoiding nuclear war and cautious of allowing local wars to turn into major conflicts with their risks of escalation. He doubts that the new nuclear powers will be willing to give up their arsenals without a fundamental shift in what he calls the "moral environment," which he does see as forthcoming. Moreover, in looking at the decades since the end of the Cold War, Karaganov sees a dangerous transition in NATO from a defensive alliance into an instrument for out-of-area intervention. In the context of Russian weakness, NATO intervened against Yugoslavia in 1999 over Kosovo. But with Russia's recovery, such a course of action is now unlikely. "Now that Russia has restored its capability, such a move would be unthinkable."[41] Instead, NATO is now involved in more distant out-of-area operations, which carry their own risks of escalation.

Against what Karaganov labels as "antinuclear mythology," he posits a hard-headed realism which rejects the ideas that nuclear arms reductions by the major powers will convince lesser powers to give up their nuclear arms, or convince other states threatened by outside powers or internal instability to give up nuclear weapons. Such arrangements might be in the interests of the two powers but cannot be justified by some supposed state of moral transcendence. States must act in their own interests in the absence of an international regime preventing the intervention of other powers. Libya's giving up the goal of nuclear weapons after the U.S.-led coalition's campaign against Iraq did not protect that state from external intervention into what was a civil war. The presence of nuclear weapons imposes restraint. It did so upon the Soviet Union when it possessed conventional superiority in Europe during the Cold War. In the post-Cold War period, it has been the compensation for Russia's weakness in conventional forces in the west and east.

> Were it not for the powerful nuclear (especially tactical) armaments, many in Russia would be alarmed over the growing potential of the Chinese general-purpose armed forces, and the specifics of certain military exercises whose scenarios include offensives stretching to hundreds and even more than one thousand kilometers.[42]

What Karaganov describes here is the geostrategic concept underlining Russia's current position in

Eurasia. On the one hand, Russian strategic nuclear weapons deter the United States and NATO from adventures at Russia's expense and provide China with an element of security that permits it to play the role of economic engine of Asia without the risk of American military intervention against it. At the same time, Russia's tactical nuclear weapons deter China from intervention in the Russian Far East and Siberia. This view certainly can be seen as providing Russia with some immediate security and even some leverage on its periphery. But it does not deal with a future where nuclear weapons might lose their deterrent capability in the face of more advanced conventional weapons, which was the prospect that Nikolai Spassky mentioned in June 2009.

Karaganov ended his essay with a distinctly Russian perspective on Global Zero, which he labeled a myth and a harmful one at that, which could unleash the dogs of war. Russia experienced two utopian visions in the 20th century. The first came with the Bolshevik Revolution and the promise of building worldwide socialism; the second occurred in 1991 with the impulse to dismantle the Soviet Union and replace it overnight with a democratic, capitalist Russia. Both dreams had tragic consequences. Contemporary Russians will not be swayed by the idealism of Global Zero. Russia can and will pursue arms control agreements that serve its national interests by making "the situation in this field more transparent, and also by building confidence between the great powers and their ability to work together." Karaganov rejects Global Zero and proposes another avenue: "To launch an international discussion about the role of military force, including nuclear weapons, in the contemporary world." Such a discussion might just conclude that nuclear weapons did have a civilizing purpose.[43]

Such sentiments did not preclude support for START III, which was waiting for ratification by both states' legislative bodies, but it did mean that there was a fundamental disconnect over where arms control and bilateral relations would go after ratification. On April 23, 2010, Karaganov endorsed ratification of START as a bilateral agreement, while restating his opposition to any multilateral move towards a nuclear-free world. "Work on the document and its signing normalized bilateral relations and made continuation of bilateral interaction and rapprochement all the more probable."[44] The treaty would lead to the dismantling of "surplus weapons," with the strategic offensive nuclear arsenals of both powers being reduced by one third. "Ratification of the document by the U.S. Senate and the Russian Federal Assembly will make the situation somewhat more stable."[45] Russia got what it could get from the negotiation. It did not make any progress towards a European Security Treaty, which President Medvedev had proposed in 2008. Washington did agree to use its influence to support the concept. Nor was there any meaningful progress made on the issue of European missile defense. Nor was there any movement in limiting U.S. efforts to develop conventional strategic strike systems. Progress in those areas was simply precluded by the existing political balance in the U.S. Senate.[46]

Karaganov even spoke positively of the follow-on nuclear summit in Washington as a valuable step towards limiting nuclear proliferation, which was, because of Russia's geostrategic location, a matter of utmost importance. But Karaganov painted a picture of proliferation which was already under way, and spoke of a need to control the process. In a dynamic international situation, Karaganov sees an absence of new concepts for a strategic order. The Obama administration's fixation on Global Zero was a manifestation of a failure of political logic. No nuclear power was likely to give up its arsenal. Russia could support efforts to reinforce nonproliferation and take part in the struggle against nuclear terrorism. But Global Zero was not part of the solution to current geostrategic instability. Indeed, pursuing it was likely to increase that instability. Karaganov went on to explain:

> The Nuclear Zero concept is an anachronism. No owner of nuclear weapons will ever part with them. It is a sheer impossibility, technically and politically. In the meantime, this anti-nuclear movement is actually harmful. First, it might result in reduction of nuclear arsenals to a dangerously low level and in negotiations over reduction of nonstrategic nuclear weapons. Second, it distracts the international community from the search for new ways to ensure peace and stability.[47]

Karaganov returned to his assumption about the amorality of nuclear weapons and repeated the point that their very destructive power made them instruments which deterred and prevented wars. The fear of mass destruction had inhibited actors during the Cold War. Since its end, NATO and the United States have shown a continuing willingness to intervene militarily in out-of-area conflicts, which increases international instability. Russia's geostrategic location, potentially near such conflicts, carries serious risks:

> Geopolitically, Russia is in trouble. Its modernization is impaired by corruption and wishes on the part of the population and the elites to be given some time to recover from niceties of the Soviet era. The situation being what it is, elimination of nuclear arsenals is tantamount to suicide. After all, nuclear arsenals are

the main guarantee of Russia's security and the main source of its political and even economic positions in the world.[48]

And it was this profound asymmetry that undercut U.S.-Russian cooperation in seeking Global Zero. The United States wants to return to a time before the first Soviet atomic bomb test on August 29, 1949. America in a world of Global Zero hopes it would achieve invulnerability, even after the interconnectedness of the global order had demonstrated its inherent vulnerability on 9/11. Russia, in all its manifestations and with all its territorial extent, has never adopted a myth of national invulnerability. The last 2 decades have left Karaganov responding to a very different imperative: the need for international discourse regarding an emerging international order which will be very different from what we have experienced, and regarding the role which all forms of military power will play in that order to enhance stability.

Rejecting Global Zero while promoting the ratification of START III, left Russian analysts with the immediate problem of enhancing strategic stability in the increasingly complex international environment in which Russia found itself. The discussions that followed in 2010 and 2011 focused on maintaining nuclear deterrence as the prospects of NATO-Russian cooperation on a joint missile defense system declined. More and more, Russia came to focus on the role of its entire nuclear arsenal in the absence of a program of modernization of conventional forces. Andrei Kokoshin, former First Deputy Minister of Defense, former head of the Defense Council, former head of the Security Council, and member of the state Duma, took the opportunity to emphasize the *real* origins of Rus-

36

sia's deterrence capabilities, not the testing of the first atomic bomb in 1949, but the detonation of RDS-57, the Soviet Union's first thermonuclear weapon, in November 1955. Marking the 55th anniversary of the testing of that device with a yield of 1.6 megatons, Kokoshin stated: "Systems and means of nuclear deterrence for the foreseeable future will remain the keystone of our security."[49] Kokoshin went on to mention the pride he felt regarding his efforts within the Russian Ministry of Defense and national security apparatus to ensure the modernization of Russia's nuclear forces in the 1990s. Furthermore, he observed that there appeared to be no alternative to nuclear deterrence even in the distant future. Russia would have to maintain its nuclear triad.[50]

Speaking to a meeting of the Social Science section of the Russian Academy of Sciences in Moscow in June 2011, Kokoshin drew upon materials from his 2009 study of *Strategic Stability, Past and Present* to call for the integration of experts from various backgrounds in the study of problems of national security, especially the problem of a reliable and convincing nuclear deterrent. Outlining foreign experience in this area, Kokoshin called for cooperation among scholars and experts in the various scientific, technical, political, and strategic aspects of the problem. Such an approach would be necessary to ensure a reliable nuclear deterrent and global and regional strategic stability. The objective of this effort would be to develop an asymmetric and indestructible response even in case the United States went ahead with a global missile defense system and sought to achieve a breakthrough in the development of offensive armaments.[51]

CONTEMPORARY THREATS AND NUCLEAR WEAPONS: THE RUSSIAN PERSPECTIVE — CONTINENTAL, GLOBAL, AND REGIONAL

Russia is a continental power with enormous natural resources but declining technological capabilities and a serious demographic crisis that is most serious in its Far Eastern domains between Chita and Vladivostok. Its threat environment is largely defined by its own periphery and the instability associated with the collapse of the USSR and the emergence there of states that are weak or hostile to the Russian Federation. It has sought to compensate for its relative weakness by geopolitical engagement across Eurasia through arrangements like the Commonwealth of Independent States (CIS), the NATO-Russia Charter, the Shanghai Cooperation Organization (SCO), the Collective Security Treaty Organization (CSTO), and the BRICS (Brazil, Russia, India, China, and South Africa) colloquium, the latter having held a summit in April 2011 in Senya in Hainan, China.[52] Russia has pursued strategic arms reductions with the United States and cooperates in nonproliferation efforts. As Nikolai Zlobin has recently pointed out, however, the current international system is deeply unstable.

Russia's elite sees very low risk of an intentional use of a core strategic arsenal against Russia — deterrence at the bilateral U.S.-Russian level still works with regard to 5th generation warfare (nuclear), offensive systems still have a sufficiently high level of survivability to ensure deterrence against a marginal ABM system, while Russia pushes its own ABM development in the S-500 which is supposed to enter the prototype stage in 2012.[53] Russia is in the process of rearming its triad with more advanced systems —

achieving great progress in surface-to-surface (S-to-S) ICBMS (Topol [SS-25], Topol-M [SS-27], and RS-24 Yars missiles), but encountering serious delays in development of the SLBM solid-fuel system RSM-56 (Bulava) for *Borea*-class ballistic missile submarine (SSBN). Additionally, it has announced plans for a stealth-like manned bomber (PAK DA) for deployment by 2025. The Russian Navy is pursuing the acquisition of a new, liquid-fueled SLBM, which is supposed to be capable of carrying 10-15 warheads. "Liner," which was first test-fired in May 2011, was originally reported to be a modernized "Sineva," but shortly thereafter press reports confirmed it was a new heavy, liquid-fueled SLBM that was twice as powerful as the solid-fueled Bulava.[54]

Aleksandr' Khramchikhin discussed the development of this new missile as part of an ongoing competition between solid-fuel and liquid-fuel missile design bureaus and warned of the destabilizing consequences of pursuing this line of development under START III, since it would feed the paranoia between Russia and the West.[55] These systems are expected to be able to penetrate even more advanced ABM systems.[56] Aleksei Arbatov has written critically about the risks of pursuing heavy, liquid-fueled ICBMs with multiple warheads and based in silos under START III because of its impact on the development of U.S. missile defense and strategic nuclear forces, but he did not examine the implications of a submarine-launched heavy missile fitted to the existing *Delta*-class SSBNs.[57]

Arbatov's point, however, remains valid. Nuclear Reset depends upon the enhancement of strategic stability and the avoidance of moves that look like efforts to achieve a strategic first-strike potential with nuclear or precision-conventional weapons. Strategic precision-strike systems are, however, still under development. They include U.S. prompt global strike capabilities based on conventional warheads for an ICBM/SLBM or an advanced hypersonic cruise missile. Senator Kerry's report on the START III Treaty discussed Russian concerns about strategic conventional precision strikes as manifest in the Treaty's preamble, "Mindful of the impact of conventionally armed ICBMs and SLBMs on strategic stability, . . ." and included a statement on Russian concerns about strategic stability in case of the deployment of large numbers of such systems and assurances from U.S. officials that such a program was only under development, would not be aimed at Russia, and would not affect strategic stability for the duration of the treaty to 2020.[58]

There do exist, however, usable conventional capabilities that can be applied in local conflicts to achieve operational-strategic results via revolution in military affairs (RMA)-based, precision-strike forces via no-contact warfare or warfare of the 6th generation. Kosovo served as a case study with variations in Afghanistan, Iraq (initial campaigns), and most recently Libya, where effects-based operations and network-centric warfare are applied to achieve rapid decision. Russian conventional weakness makes this point of paramount importance and is currently driving renewed effort at military reform, or New look (Novyi Oblik), under Minister Serdiukov and Chief of the General Staff Makarov. This New Look emerged after the Georgian-Soviet conflict of August 2008 over South Ossetia and Abkhazia that has been called "The Tanks of August," suggesting the 4th generation of warfare character (mass-mechanized forces) of that conflict.[59] Makarov and Serdiukov are pushing for a brigade-based professional force capable of network-centric warfare to be developed over the next decade. It is unclear whether this will be achieved. Growing recognition of low-end asymmetric counters by insurgents-terrorists to 5th generation warfare has led to discussions of a new look at the relationship between terrorism, insurgency, and conflict escalation.[60] The lesson in the case of out-of-area intervention by Western powers with advanced conventional capabilities (6th generation warfare) is that nuclear weapons are the most reliable check against them. This led Aleksei Bogaturov in 2009 to observe that while prospects for nuclear war with the United States are low, the chances of the use of nuclear weapons are higher:

> The likelihood of a nuclear war with the U.S. is estimated, by and large, as fairly low, while the likelihood of the use of nuclear weapons by various countries of the world, including the United States and, probably, Russia itself, is now higher than 15-17 years ago. Admittedly, what is implied is a limited use of such weapons.[61]

Bogaturov specifically mentioned a new generation of low-yield nuclear weapons playing a role in such operations. Limited nuclear first strikes with nonstrategic forces as a means of de-escalating local wars have been acknowledged as part of Russia's deterrence posture where Russian and allied interests or Russian statehood are threatened. The *Russian Military Doctrine of 2010* stated that nuclear weapons would be used: "In reply to the use of nuclear and other mass destruction weapons against it and (or) its allies, as well as in reply to a large-scale aggression with the use of conventional weapons in situations critical for the national security of the Russian Federation."[62]

These threats are seen as lying on the Russian periphery and are connected to instability in the near abroad and NATO expansion. Strategic exercises with an anti-NATO focus since Kosovo (Zapad 1999 to Zapad 2009) have emphasized Russia's limited conventional force capabilities and a nuclear option of first use to de-escalate an intervention on the periphery. Russian military and political specialists treat Operation ALLIED FORCE (the air campaign against Yugoslavia) as a miscalculation by Allied leaders on the feasibility of a short, decisive air campaign to achieve decision without the combat employment of ground forces, which carried grave risks of escalation into a wider conflict. The Russians foresaw the same problem with the decision to impose a no-fly zone over Libya and the employment of air power to protect the civilian population. President Medvedev responded to Security Council Resolution 1973 by urging the international community to cooperate in ending the conflict, but stated: "We will not participate in any of the no-fly zone operations [in Libya], we will not send any troops, if, God forbid, this operation goes on the ground, which I cannot rule out."[63]

China represents an ambiguity in the nuclear equation. The best case is China as a regional power with the capacity to organize a zone of influence in the Far East to counterbalance U.S.-Japanese interests, in which China seeks Russian support as giving it strategic depth. The SCO as both anti-Islamic terror and anti-hegemon policy serves this purpose. Ideally, this would involve collaboration of the Russian Federation, China, and India. Russia needs Indian support to avoid the trap of serving as junior partner to China in the case of a Sino-U.S. conflict, where Russia would be drawn in. It sees a Sino-Indian conflict as detrimental to Russian interests. Worst cases are a Sino-American deal at Russia's expense, where China can effectively penetrate and woo away the Russian Far East to Lake Baikal in a deal over spheres of influence; and a Sino-American confrontation over the integration of Taiwan into the PRC, where the United States would be forced to use nuclear weapons. Moreover, an American policy to contain China as a rival, given the shifting balance of economic power, could create an even greater role for nuclear weapons with associated risks of conflict and Russia being drawn in as a pawn between the two rivals.

The Russian military assessment of China's military potential has stressed the evolutionary nature of that transformation. In this analysis, the Chinese mass military has been modernized but is far from becoming a 6th generation force. Therefore, 5th generation capability trumps 4th generation numbers, so long as China is not a geostrategic partner of the United States as existed in the 1980s. Russia's fear is that Chinese military modernization will reach a plateau where Russian arms and technology assistance will no longer be needed for sustained modernization.[64] Russian arms deals with India have taken on the character of a bet against such a development. The Sukhoi aircraft plant at Komsomolsk-an-Amure is morphing from producer of aircraft (SU-27M) for the PRC to partner with Hindustan Aeronautics Limited (HAL) in the development of the 5th generation fighter (FGFA/PAK FA), which began taxi tests in January 2012. Vostok 2010 was a major exercise testing the New Look for Russia's conventional forces, but it ended with a simulated nuclear first-strike.[65]

This is supposed to be the exact focus of Vostok-2010.[66] The New Look military which the Ministry of Defense has set out to create via a brigade-based ground force capable of launching precision strikes and conducting network-centric warfare faces a particular challenge in Siberia and the Far East, where Chinese military modernization has converted the PLA from a mass industrial army built to fight people's war to a force seeking to rearm as an advanced conventional force and able to conduct its own version of network-centric warfare. Until 2010, informed Russian defense journalists still spoke of the PLA as a mass industrial army seeking niche advanced conventional capabilities. Looking at the threat environment that was assumed to exist under Zapad 2009, defense journalist Dmitri Litovkin spoke of Russian forces confronting three distinct types of military threats:

> [In the West] an opponent armed to NATO standards in the Georgian-Russian confrontation over South Ossetia last year. In the eastern strategic direction, Russian forces would likely face a multi-million-man army with a traditional approach to the conduct of combat: linear deployments with large concentrations of manpower and fire power on different axes. In the southern strategic direction Russian forces expect to confront irregular forces and sabotage groups fighting a partisan war against "the organs of Federal authority," i.e., Internal troops, the border patrol, and the FSB.[67]

By the spring of 2011, a number of those involved in bringing about the New Look were speaking of a PLA that was moving rapidly towards a high-tech conventional force with its own understanding of network-centric warfare.[68] Moreover, the PLA conducted a major exercise, "Stride-2009," which looked like a rehearsal for military intervention against Central Asia and/or Russia to some Russian observers. PLA units engaged in strategic-operational redeployments of units from Shenyang, Lanzhou, Jinan, and Guangzhou military commands by air and rail movement.[69] Aleksandr' Khramchikhin in the fall of 2009 warned that China and its military were well on the way to becoming a real military superpower combining numbers and advanced technology. The PLA no longer needed to go hat-in-hand to the Russian defense industry for advanced weapons but was set upon building its own in partnership with other powers. Looking at the geostrategic situation in the Far East and Central Asia, he warned:

> I repeat once more: it is possible to assert that the leadership of the PRC and the PLA high-command are seriously considering the possibility of conducting in the foreseeable future offensive actions against Russia and the states of Central Asia. To some degree, precisely such a scenario of war is considered the most probable. At the same time, operations for the forceful seizure of Taiwan have been removed from the order of the day.[70]

Speaking of Russia's deployment of two newly-organized brigades along the Russian-Chinese border on the Irkutsk-Chita axis, Lieutenant-General Vladimir Valentinovich Chirkin, the recently appointed commander of the Siberian Military District, stated that the brigades were deployed there to counter the presence of five PLA combined arms armies across the border. From 2003 to 2007, Chirkin commanded an army in the Siberian Military District. On the rationale for the deployment, Chirkin stated: "We are obligated to keep troops there because on the other side of the border are five Chinese armies and we cannot ignore that operational direction." He added that the Ministry of Defense intended to develop an army headquarters for command and control of the brigades.[71] In a related report, Chirkin described the PLA forces across the border as composed of three divisions and 10 tank, mechanized, and infantry brigades, which he described as not little but also "not a strike force." As to the role of the new Russian brigades, Chirkin described them as part of a deterrent force aimed as a friendly reminder to the PRC: "Despite the friendly relations with China our army command understands that friendship is possible only with strong countries, that is, [those] who can quiet a friend down with a conventional or nuclear club."[72]

The gamble on the nature of future war described by A. Kondrat'ev in supporting the development of network-centric warfare capabilities comes down to the issue of Russia's capacity to arm, create, train, deploy, and maintain in combat readiness forces capable of conducting advanced conventional warfare. In the absence of such forces, the deterrence equation is reduced to the credibility of the nuclear option in deterring conventional attacks. Given the economic and demographic realities of Siberia and the Russian Far East, Russia seeks by nonmilitary means to preclude the emergence of a Chinese military threat. However, Russian observers are also aware of the fact that an imminent military threat from Beijing can emerge from regional instability which is beyond Russia's unilateral means to control. As the most recent *Russian Military Doctrine of 2010* explains, nuclear weapons remain the primary instrument of deterrence against both nuclear and conventional attacks upon Russia and in defense of Russian interests, territorial integrity, and sovereignty.[73] The doctrine does not explicitly declare that Russia will use nuclear weapons in preemptive attacks against such threats, as had been discussed by senior members of the Security Council in the fall of 2009, but it leaves the decision to use such weapons in the hands of the President of the Russian Federation. The context of such use, however, is defined by the nature of the challenges and threats that Russia faces across Eurasia. A second classified document, *The Foundations of State Policy in the Area of Nuclear Deterrence to 2020*, which was issued at the same time as the *Military Doctrine*, has been leaked in part to the mass media. These parts describe two types of threats that could lead to the use of nuclear weapons: 1) attacks upon vital economic and political structures, early warning systems, national command and control, and nuclear weapons systems, all of which would seem to envision a U.S.-led NATO threat involving conventional forces capable of conducting global strikes against such targets; and, 2) an invasion by an enemy's ground units of Russian territory in which Russia's armed forces fail to stop their progress deep into the country through conventional means, all of which suggests more closely an assault by the PLA against the Russian Far East.[74]

The first conceptual threat resembles one popularized by General-Major Vladimir Slipchenko in his discussions of 6th generation warfare and no-contact warfare on the model of NATO's campaign against Kosovo but applied on a global scale.[75] The second one, which was not contained in the 2000 version of Russian military doctrine, is quite new, reflecting what the Russian military recognizes is an emerging threat from the PRC. Relying upon nuclear deterrence in such a conflict with China is not considered by some Russian military observers to be a viable course of action. Khramchikhin has expressed this view in a debate with Aleksei Arbatov, one of Russia's most respected commentators on nuclear issues and a strong believer in the continued utility of nuclear deterrence even in the face of the spread of advanced conventional capabilities. Khramchikhin's answer has been to call nuclear deterrence an illusion. The illusion arises from Russia's general weakness in conventional forces, its limited mobility in supporting forces in distant frontiers, and the inappropriateness of nuclear strikes for resolving limited conflicts over border issues. Advanced conventional capabilities will soon make possible global conventional strikes with the effects of nuclear weapons. In the case of China, Khramchikhin argues that there is a great need to protect Siberia and the Far East as key sources of critical raw materials and energy for the future development of the country, but demographic weakness, obsolete infrastructure, and weak conventional forces make that task nearly impossible, with nuclear deterrence in this context a shallow hope. Khramchikhin leaves one with the impression that the situation confronting Russia in the Far East is not too different from that confronting Pakistan, given India's development of advanced conventional capabilities to strike towards Islamabad. In neither case does nuclear retaliation become a solution for confronting slowly mobilizing conventional forces in the hands of a more developed and more populous opponent.[76]

All these strictly military calculations cannot deal with the full dynamic of threats confronting Russia. The wild card in the nuclear environment is the threat of what Andrei Kokoshin identified as mega-terrorism, the mass casualties and destruction from terrorist actions like that of 9/11 which could drive political-military responses in directions not foreseen by political-military planners.[77] Kokoshin includes weapons of mass effect (WME) as well as weapons of mass destruction (WMD) in this calculus. Russia will collaborate in regional efforts to reduce terrorist threats and retain Russian influence. It has good reason to see nuclear proliferation as dangerous to Russia's own strategic situation and to the current international system and will cooperate in endeavors to reduce such risks so long as they do not result in the use of force, which would further destabilize the global system and regional security structures. Mega-terrorism poses a particularly major risk in the relationship between Pakistan and India. Such an event could set off a conflict that would be difficult for the international community to moderate and could drive external intervention and a concomitant risk of nuclear escalation.

Iran represents a particularly difficult problem because of its involvement in supporting anti-Israeli terrorism, Israeli fears of Iranian acquisition of nuclear weapons, and the deployment of U.S. and coalition forces in both Iraq and Afghanistan, which could transform any limited strikes against Iranian nuclear facilities into a larger regional conflict on Russia's periphery, thus impacting the Caucasus and Central Asia and giving new momentum to Islamic extremism globally. At present, as we watch the unfolding of the "Arab Revolutions" across North Africa and the Middle East, this particular problem has to be reassessed. Commenting on the United Nations (UN) Security Council resolution for the imposition of a no-fly zone against Libya, some Russian commentators have wondered whether Muammar Gaddafi's decision to give up Libya's chemical and nuclear weapons programs in December 2003 was not short-sighted, pointing to the fact that North Korea has openly tested nuclear weapons and ballistic missiles and engaged in repeated provocations against South Korea without facing any use of force against it. Mikhail Lukanin, the defense correspondent for *Trud*, stated flatly: "They would not have touched Gaddafi if he had built an atomic bomb." Lukanin listed other states which might be tempted to acquire nuclear weapons in the aftermath of the Arab Revolution and included Saudi Arabia because of the changes in the balance of power in the Middle East and the enhanced position of Iran.[78]

In April 2011 in the midst of the initial response to NATO intervention in Libya, the Russian press published an extended examination of the possible course and outcome of an Israeli-Iranian War. Drawing heavily upon the 2009 study by the Center for Strategic and International Studies in Washington, DC, regarding an Israeli preemptive strike at Iran's nuclear program, the author invited Russian specialists to comment on the course and outcome of such a possible conflict. The estimated losses by both sides from missile attacks using nuclear and chemical weapons stood at 20 million Iranian casualties and 800,000 Israeli casualties. The Russian experts did not exclude the possibility of a more protracted conflict, in which both sides employed indirect means and surrogate forces, which they viewed as a possibility if Iran did create its own nuclear forces. They noted the paradox of self-deterrence, when both sides have nuclear arsenals. "The creation of nuclear weapons by Iran could actually be a positive development. When both countries possess them, this creates a powerful deterrence factor and most likely the leaders of both Israel and Iran could be deterred from a direct military conflict."[79]

The implications of increased nuclear proliferation for Russian national security will be a topic of intense debate among the Russian national security elite. It is very likely to color the Russian approach to negotiations on reductions in, and confidence-building measures pertaining to, nonstrategic nuclear weapons. The last few months have not lent much hope of bilateral or multilateral progress on arms control in the areas of missile defense, nonstrategic nuclear weapons, or conventional forces in Europe. The very complexity and interconnections of these issues makes progress very unlikely.

CURRENT U.S.-RUSSIAN DISCUSSIONS ON NONSTRATEGIC NUCLEAR WEAPONS AND MISSILE DEFENSES AS SEEN FROM MOSCOW

With the ratification of START III by the U.S. Congress and the Russian parliament, nonstrategic nuclear weapons became a topic of intense discussions between Washington and Moscow. Rose Gottemoeller, Assistant Secretary of State for Verification, Compliance, and Implementation, stated in January 2011 that the topic was now on the agenda of U.S.-Russian relations and pointed to studies by nongovernmental groups in the United States and Russia that addressed the topic.[80]

Governmental groups, notably NATO member governments, have come forward with their own proposals regarding U.S. and Russian nonstrategic nuclear weapons in Europe. In early February 2011, Lithuanian Defense Minister Rasa Jukneviciene announced that Russia had deployed tactical nuclear weapons in Kaliningrad Oblast' and called upon "the world powers" to begin negotiations to ensure their removal.

Jukneviciene said that Lithuanian national interests demanded the removal of such weapons since they posed a threat to "our very existence."[81] Recently, the Four-Plus-Six Group put forward a proposal by NATO members to increase transparency in U.S. and Russia nonstrategic nuclear weapons, which was submitted in a "so-called 'nonpaper'" by Germany, the Netherlands, Norway, and Poland, and endorsed by Belgium, the Czech Republic, Iceland, Luxembourg, and Slovenia, and which highlights this difference among NATO members. The proposal outlines a series of transparency and confidence-building measures, which include:

> 1) Use the NATO-Russia Council (NRC) as the primary framework for transparency and confidence-building efforts concerning tactical nuclear weapons in Europe; 2) Exchange information about U.S. and Russian tactical nuclear weapons, including numbers, locations, operational status, and command arrangements, as well as level of warhead storage security; 3) Agree on a standard reporting formula for tactical nuclear weapons inventories; 4) Consider voluntary notifications of movement of tactical nuclear weapons; 5) Exchange visits by military officials [presumably to storage locations]; 6) Exchange conditions and requirements for gradual reductions of tactical nuclear weapons in Europe, including clarifying the number of weapons that have been eliminated and/or stored as a result of the 1991-1992 Presidential Nuclear Initiatives (PNIs); and, 7) Hold a NRC seminar on tactical nuclear weapons in the first quarter of 2012 in Poland.[82]

It is noteworthy that this proposal did not include among its sponsors or supporters either of the two other NATO members with nuclear weapons, Britain, and France, or the three Baltic States.

A deal over a joint missile defense system might have provided a basis for such a choice but a joint NATO-Russia system is not in the cards. In a recent interview in Moscow, Assistant Secretary of Defense Alexander Vershbow spoke of a solution for the problem of missile defense involving two separate but parallel missile defense systems, which would coordinate their work, rather than a common system.[83] He also held out the possibility of creating two structures for missile defense cooperation. One would be a center for the integration of ground-based and space-based radar and sensor data from NATO and Russian sources, and the second center would be involved in planning and coordinating missile defense.

However, there was little enthusiasm in Moscow for such ideas after the announcement that the United States planned to extend its European Phased Adaptive Approach (EPAA) to the Black Sea littoral by including Turkey and Rumania in the system. Russian press coverage of Turkey's membership came as an unpleasant surprise to Moscow because the EPAA radar component would reduce the possibility of cooperation in the sharing of radar and sensor data, given the close cooperation that would be expected between the U.S. radar in Turkey and that deployed in Israel.[84] The decision to deploy missile defense interceptors in Rumania did not create as much concern because their characteristics did not make them capable of intercepting warheads.[85] Vladimir Kozin, a frequent commentator on missile defense and nonstrategic nuclear missiles, called attention to the development of sea-based Aegis systems for deployment in the Adriatic, Aegean, and Black Seas as a developing threat to Russia's strategic nuclear forces. He called for the removal of U.S. tactical nuclear forces from Europe and linked to that the goal of limiting the deployment of sea-based missile defense systems to strictly defined regions of the world's oceans.[86]

CONCLUSIONS

Russia is not in a position to enter into meaningful arms control negotiations at this time. The successors to the leadership tandem in Moscow will wait and see how the situation develops in Washington, meanwhile pursuing completion of Russia's 2020 armament plan, which is supposed to modernize strategic and tactical nuclear forces and create the foundation for a modern conventional military, which embraces command, control, communications, computers, and intelligence surveillance and reconnaissance (C4ISR). Given the past failure of Russian armament programs, there is no guarantee that Russia will be in a stronger position in 2020, but there are no political incentives to seek a general deal with Washington or to embrace multilateral negotiations where Russia might find itself isolated. Russia can continue to avoid the dilemma of choosing between Washington and Beijing, time does appear to be the friend of a power like Russia, which most of all needs stability for itself and Eurasia.

ENDNOTES - CHAPTER 1

1. Jacob W. Kipp, "Presidential Elections and the Future of U.S.-Russian Relations," in Stephen J. Blank, ed., *Prospects for U.S.-Russian Security Cooperation*, Carlisle, PA: Strategic Studies Institute, U.S. Army War College, 2009, pp. 45-97.

2. Peter Baker, "Obama Offered Deal to Russia in Secret Letter," *The New York Times*, March 2, 2009.

3. "The Global Zero movement," available from *www.globalzero.org/en/about-campaign*.

4. Vladimir Dobrovol'skii, "Global Zero prizyvaet Medvedeva i Obamu k unichtozheniiu iadernogo oruzhiia," *RIA Novisti*, March 24, 2009.

5. Michael D. Shear and Scott Wilson, "Obama, Medvedev Pledge Cooperation," *The Washington Post*, April 2, 2009.

6. The Treaty between the United States of America and the Russian Federation on Measures for the Further Reduction and Limitation of Strategic Offensive Arms, "Remarks by President Barack Obama," Hradcany Square, Prague, Czech Republic, Washington, DC: The White House, April 5, 2009, available from *www.whitehouse.gov/the_press_office/Remarks-By-President-Barack-Obama-In-Prague-As-Delivered/*.

7. "The Global Zero movement."

8. Dmitry Petrov, "Nuclear Zero aye nay abstained," *Rossiia*, June 6-14, 2009.

9. *Ibid.*

10. *Ibid.*

11. *Ibid.*

12. "Opening Day Statement from Global Zero Leaders," *Global Zero movement*, February 2-4, 2010, available from *www.globalzero.org/en/opening-day-statement-global-zero-leaders*.

13. *Ibid.*

14. "The New START Treaty and Protocol," Washington, DC: The White House, April 8, 2010, available from *www.whitehouse.gov/blog/2010/04/08/new-start-treaty-and-protocol*.

15. Oleg Nikiforov, "Bumazhnyi tigr ili real'naia ugroza," *Nezavisimoe voennoe obozrenie*, February 5, 2010.

16. On the status of the "New Look" in Russian defense policy as it relates to the modernization of conventional forces follow-

ing the August 2008 Russo-Georgian War, see Roger McDermott, *Russia's Military Transformation: Implications for NATO*, Washington, DC: Jamestown Foundation, 2011; and Timothy Thomas, *Recasting the Red Star: Russia Forges Tradition and Technology through Toughness*, Ft. Leavenworth, KS: Foreign Military Studies Office, 2011.

17. Olga Bozheva, "Antivoennaia doktrina," *Moskovskii komsomolets*, February 8, 2010.

18. Aleksandr Khramchikhin, "Esli zavtra voina . . .Vtoraia koreiskaia," *Nezavisimoe voennoe obozrenie*, February 4, 2010.

19. Andrei Terekhov, "Mudretsy NATO napomnili Moskve o Kitaiskom vyzove," *Nezavisimoe gazeta*, February 12, 2010.

20. Vladimir Kuzar', "SSha - KNR: Vyzov na duel'?" *Krasnaia zvezda*, February 10, 2010.

21. "Dmitry Medvedev and Barack Obama will meet in Prague to sign a new strategic arms reduction treaty," The President of Russia, March 26, 2010, available from *eng.kremlin.ru*.

22. "Key Facts about the New START Treaty," The White House, March 26, 2010.

23. Nikolai Surkov, "Moscow and Washington Close to Agreement," *Nezavisimaia gazeta*, March 24, 2010.

24. "Rossiia i SShA pokazali primer drugim," *Nezavisimaia gazeta*, March 29, 2010.

25. Denis Tel'manov and Anastasiia Novikova, "V novom dogovore ob SNV 'podedila druzhba'," *Gazeta*, March 29, 2010.

26. Nikolai Snezhkov, "Vnimanie, na START," *Vremia novostei*, March 31, 2010.

27. Fedor Lukianov, "Poslednyi dogovor," *Vremia novostei*, March 29, 2010.

28. Melor Sturua, "Kak Medveev i Obama spasli dogovor po SNV," *Izvestiia*, March 30, 2010.

29. Polina Khimshiashvili and Natal'ia Kostenko, "Sokratiat minimal'no," *Vedomosti*, March 29, 2010 .

30. Sergei Lavrov, "The New Strategic Arms Reduction Treaty in the Global Security Matrix: The Political Dimension," *International Affairs*, No. 4, 2010, p. 16.

31. *Ibid.*, p. 2.

32. *Ibid.*, p. 4.

33. *Ibid.*, pp. 10-11.

34. *Ibid.*, p. 11.

35. *Ibid.*

36. *Ibid.*, p. 18.

37. Sergei Karaganov "Global Zero and Common Sense," *Russia in Global Affairs*, No. 2, 2010, p. 26.

38. *Ibid.*, p. 27.

39. *Ibid.*, p. 28.

40. *Ibid.*

41. *Ibid.*, p. 29.

42. *Ibid.*, p. 30.

43. *Ibid.*, p. 34.

44. "START Promotes Russian-American Cooperation and Rapprochement: Nuclear Free World Is a Dangerous Concept that Ought to be Abandoned," *Rossiiskaia gazeta*, April 23, 2011.

45. *Ibid.*

46. *Ibid.*

47. *Ibid.*

48. *Ibid.*

49. V. L., "Bomba spravliaet iubilei," *Nezavisimoe voennoe obozrenie*, November 26, 2010.

50. *Ibid.*

51. "Iz Rossiiskoi akademii nauk: Asimmetrichno i nerazopitel'no," *Krasnaia Zvezda*, June 28, 2011. On Kokoshin's view on strategic stability, see A. Kokoshin, *Obespechenie strategicheskoi stabil'nosti v proshlom, i nastoiashchem: Teoritecheskie i prikladnye voprosy*, Moscow, Russia: Krasand, 2009.

52. Nataliia Ermolik, "BRIKS Nabiraet oboroty," *Krasnaia zvezda*, April 14, 2011, p. 1. Brazil, Russia, India, China (BRIC) officially became BRICS in 2011 when South Africa joined the BRIC summit meeting in Sanya. While seen as an ad hoc group lacking common interests, these powers do share common views on United Nations (UN) Security Council reform and on the air intervention in Libya.

53. "Russia set to finish development of new air defense system," *RIA Novosti*, September 16, 2009, available from *en.rian.ru/mlitary_news/20090916/156150066.html*.

54. Aleksandr Emel'ianenkov, "Za 'Sinevoi' pustili 'Lainer'," *Rossiiskaia gazeta*, May 25, 2011.

55. Aleksandr Khramchikhin, "Perspektivnaia MBR — zhidkostnaia ili tverdotoplivaia," *Nezavisimoe voennoe obozrenie*, June 17, 2011.

56. Vladimir Popovkin, "Perspektivy perevooruzheniia vooruzhennykh sil Rossiiskooi Federatsii," *Rossiiskoe voennoe obozrenie*, March 2011, pp. 15-20; and Viktor Litovkin, "Raketnaia nanaiskaia bor'ba," *Nezavisimoe voennoe obozrenie*, February 4, 2011, p. 1.

57. A. G. Arbatov, "Iadernaia perezahruzka i mezhdunarodnaia besposnost'," *Pol\\OLIS, Politicheskie issledovaniia*, No. 3, 2011, pp. 39-40.

58. U. S. Senate, 111th Cong., 2nd Sess., *Treaty with Russia on Reductions and Further Limitations of Strategic Offensive Arms (The New START Treaty) Report* submitted by Mr. Kerry from the Senate Foreign Relations Committee, October 1, 2010, pp. 51-53.

59. Jacob Kipp, " The Russia-Georgia Conflict as Analyzed by the Center of Analysis of Strategies and Technologies in Moscow," *Eurasia Daily Monitor*, Vol. 7, Issues: 15 and 16, available from *www.jamestown.org/single/?no_cache=1&tx_ttnews%5Bsword s%5D=8fd5893941d69d0be3f378576261ae3e&tx_ttnews%5Bany_of_ the_words%5D=Tanks%20of%20the%20august&tx_ttnews%5Btt_ news%5D=35947&tx_ttnews%5BbackPid%5D=7&cHash= 88e09810c5*; and *www.jamestown.org/single/?no_cache=1&tx_ttne ws[swords]=8fd5893941d69d0be3f378576261ae3e&tx_ttnews[any_ of_the_words]=Tanks%20of%20the%20august&tx_ttnews[tt_ news]=35951&tx_ttnews[backPid]=7&cHash=3ef1cf451f*.

60. McDermott.

61. Aleksei Bogaturov, "Russia and the USA: Equilibrium of Distrust," *Mezhdunarodnye protsessy*, Vol. VII, No. 3, 2009, p. 124.

62. "Military Doctrine of the Russian Federation," *Military News Bulletin*, May 1, 2000.

63. "Russia not to participate in no-fly zone operations in Libya—Medvedev," *RIA Novosti*, March 21, 2011, available from *en.rian.ru/world/20110321/163131709.html*.

64. A. Kondrat'ev, "Nekotorye osobenosti realizatsii kontseptsii 'setetsentricheskaia voina' v vooruzhennykh silakh KNR," *Zarubezhnoe voennoe obozrenie*, March 2010, pp. 11-17.

65. Alexander Khramchikhin, "Inadequate East," *Nezavisimoe voennoe obozrenie*, July 23-29, 2010, p. 1.

66. Alesksei Nikol'skii, "Otsenku dast 'Vostok'," *Vedomosti*, March 9, 2010.

67. Dmitri Litovkin, "Ucheniia popali v seti," *Izvestiia*, September 28, 2009.

68. A. Kondrat'ev, "Nekotorye osobennosti realizatsii kontseptsii 'setetsentricheskaia voina' v vooruzhennykh silakh KNR," *Zarubezhnoe voennoe obozrenie*, No. 3, March 2010, pp. 11-17.

69. "Ucheniia," *Zarubezhnoe voennoe obozrenie* , No. 8, July 31, 2009; and Aleksandr Khramchikhin, "Starye osnovy novoi doktriny," *Voyenno-Promyshlennyy Kuryer*, No. 6, February 17, 2010, p. 5.

70. Aleksandr Khramchikhin, "Milliony soldat plius sovremennoe vooruzhenie," *Nezavisimoe voennoe obozrenie*, October 9, 2009.

71. "Novosti," *VPK-Voennopromyshlennyi kur'er*, March 3, 2010.

72. "Russia Strengthens the Border with China," *Argumenty nedeli*, March 4-10, 2010.

73. Prezident Rossii, *Voennaia doktrina Rossiiskoi Federatsii*, February 5, 2010.

74. Vladimir Mokhov, "Osnovy natsional'noi bezopastosti," *Krasnaia zvezda*, February 6, 2010.

75. V. I. Slipchenko, *Voina budushchego*, Moscow, Russia: Izdetl'skii Tsentr nauchnykh i uchebnykh programm, 1999; and V. I. Slipchenko, *Beskontaktnye voiny*, Moscow, Russia: "Gran-Press," 2001. On the debate between Slipchenko and Makhmut Gareev over the prospects of "no-contact war" vs. mass mobilization advanced conventional war with ground forces, see Makhmut Gareev and Vladimir Slipchenko, *Future War*, Ft. Leavenworth, KS: Foreign Military Studies Office, 2007.

76. Aleksandr Khramchikhin. "Illiuziia iadernogo sderzhivaniia," *VPK Voenno-promyshlennyi kur'er*, March 24, 2010.

77. A. A. Kokoshin, *Iadernye konflikty v XXI veke: Tipy, formy, vozmozhnye uchastniki*, Moscow, Russia: Media-Press, 2003, pp. 67-76.

78. Mikhail Lukanin, "Arabskii krizis mozhet pereasti v at-omnyi," *Trud*, March 29, 2011, p. 1; and Viacheslav Tetekin, "Li-viiskii urok," *Pravda*, April 1, 2011, p. 7.

79. Sergei Turchenko, "Voiny: XXI veka: Izrail' protiv Irana, *Svobodnaia pressa*, April 17, 2011.

80. "US wants to step up dialogue with Russia on non-stra-tegic weapons," *Russia Today*, January 20, 2011, available from *rt.com/politics/russia-usa-arms-control/*.

81. Litva prizvala mirovye derzhavy nachat' peregovory or-ganixheniiu takicheskogo iadernogo oruzhiia dislotsipovannogo v Kalingradskoi oblasti," *Defens E'skress: Ezhennedelnaia lenta novostei*, February 8, 2011, available from *dlib.eastview.com.www2.lib.ku.edu:2048/browse/doc/24215096*.

82. Hans M. Kristensen, "10 NATO Countries Want More Transparency for Non-Strategic Nuclear Weapons," Washington, DC: Federation of American Scientists, April 24, 2011, available from *www.fas.org/blog/ssp/2011/04/natoproposal.php*.

83. Aleksandr Artem'ev, "Nasha ideia - dve otdel'nye sistemy PRO," *Kommersant*, September 12, 2011.

84. Aleksandr Semenov, "Amerikanskuiu PRO razmestiat v Turtsii," *Komsomol'skaia pravda*, September 3, 2011.

85. "Dar'ia Tsiliurik, SShA sovratili Rumyniiu na evro-peiskuiu PRO," *Nezavisimaia gazeta*, September 14, 2011.

86. Vladimir Kozin, "Ugroza s moria," *Krasnaia zvezda*, Sep-tember 2, 2011.

CHAPTER 2

THE RUSSIAN ARMS CONTROL AGENDA
AFTER NEW START

Steven Pifer

INTRODUCTION

With the New Strategic Arms Reduction Treaty (New START) having entered into force in February 2011, the question arose as to what would come next on the U.S.-Russian arms control agenda. As early as April 2010, President Barack Obama called for further negotiations to reduce U.S. and Russian nuclear forces below New START levels and to address nondeployed strategic warheads and nonstrategic nuclear weapons. President Dmitri Medvedev has agreed in principle to a step-by-step process of further nuclear reductions, but Moscow has shown little enthusiasm for a new round of negotiations.

This chapter examines what Russian officials were saying about next steps on the arms control agenda and possible missile defense cooperation, as of autumn 2011. It also looks at Russian concerns about conventional force disadvantages, how those concerns might affect the Russian approach to arms control, and possible incentives that Moscow may have in the medium term to explore further nuclear arms cuts.

Russian officials in 2011 said that a number of issues should be addressed in conjunction with, if not before, further nuclear arms reductions. These issues included missile defense, long-range conventional strike weapons, the fate of the Conventional Forces in Europe (CFE) Treaty, and weapons in outer space. The bundling of these questions may reflect uncertainty in Moscow as to where to go next on arms control. Russian officials also said they wanted to see how New START was implemented, and both countries faced presidential elections in 2012.

Moscow has said little about further cuts of strategic nuclear forces and virtually nothing about nonstrategic nuclear weapons — sometimes referred to as sub-strategic or tactical nuclear weapons — other than to call for the removal of U.S. nonstrategic weapons from Europe to national territory, which the Russians said should be a precondition for any negotiation on such weapons. The Russian military attaches importance to its nonstrategic arsenal, including tactical nuclear weapons, as offsetting perceived conventional force disadvantages vis-à-vis the North Atlantic Treaty Organization (NATO) and China. Some analysts suggested the Russians would not be prepared for a serious discussion of reducing nonstrategic nuclear weapons until they had a prospect of modernizing their conventional forces; it is unclear how long that will take.

At the end of 2011, the issue on the arms control agenda receiving the most attention was missile defense and whether the United States, NATO, and Russia could agree on the terms for a cooperative missile defense system for Europe. Moscow focused on the bilateral dialogue with Washington on this issue. The sides reportedly found some common ground on practical cooperation, such as transparency and a data fusion center. Washington believed that such cooperation would yield significant transparency about U.S. missile defense plans and capabilities and would assure Russia that those plans did not pose a serious threat to Russian strategic ballistic missile forces.

Moscow, however, sought a legal "guarantee" that U.S. systems would not be directed against Russian strategic forces and "criteria" regarding U.S. missile defenses that went beyond what the administration was prepared to offer—or what the Senate would be prepared to support.

If the missile defense cooperation question is resolved, it would improve prospects for new bilateral nuclear arms negotiations. Moscow has incentives to engage at some point in such negotiations. The Russians may have trouble maintaining the level of 1,550 deployed strategic warheads allowed under New START; the U.S. military will not. The treaty, moreover, will leave the United States with a sizable advantage in strategic "upload" capability. A new arms control agreement would offer Moscow the best vehicle to address these issues as well as to secure the withdrawal of U.S. nonstrategic nuclear weapons from Europe and their future limitation to U.S. territory.

Conventional forces in Europe posed an equally difficult question in 2011. Efforts during 2010 to revive the CFE Treaty stumbled over the question of host nation consent to stationing of foreign forces, which brought to the fore the status of South Ossetia and Abkhazia. Given such differences and the need to find consensus among 30 CFE Treaty parties, salvaging CFE appears a nearly hopeless task. While the Russians said they wanted a treaty regime to cover and limit conventional armed forces in Europe, they offered no workable ideas to break the impasse.

NEW START AND U.S.-RUSSIAN NUCLEAR FORCE LEVELS

New START has proved a key element of Washington's Reset policy with Moscow. The Russians appreciated the fact that the Obama administration supplanted its predecessor's approach to strategic arms control with a more traditional approach, one that provided for legally-binding limits on strategic delivery vehicles as well as strategic warheads. (The Russians had rejected the approach suggested by the George Bush administration in 2008, which would have limited only deployed strategic warheads.) Signed in April 2010, New START entered into force on February 5, 2011, following a ratification debate in the U.S. Senate that proved more difficult than anticipated. By contrast, the Russian Duma ratified New START in January 2011, not surprisingly with relative ease.

New START contains three limits. When the treaty's reductions are fully implemented by February 5, 2018, each side will be limited to no more than 1,550 deployed strategic warheads; 700 deployed strategic delivery vehicles, i.e., intercontinental ballistic missiles (ICBMs), submarine-launched ballistic missiles (SLBMs) and nuclear-capable bombers; and 800 deployed and nondeployed launchers for ICBMs and SLBMs plus nuclear-capable bombers. The sides exchanged data in February 2011 and exchanged their first data update the following September. (See Figure 2-1.)

	Treaty Limit	U.S.	Russia
Deployed Strategic Warheads	1,550	1,790	1,566
Deployed Strategic Delivery Vehicles	700	822	516
Deployed and Non-Deployed ICBM/SLBM Launchers plus Bombers	800	1,043	871

Figure 2-1. U.S. and Russian Strategic Forces, September 2011.[1]

The lower Russian numbers reflect the fact that in recent years many Russian strategic missiles have reached or exceeded their service warranty life and been retired, and the relatively modest pace at which Moscow has procured new ICBMs and SLBMs.

Nongovernmental analysts in the United States project that the Russian military will have a hard time maintaining 1,550 deployed strategic warheads and could fall to around 1,260-1,350.[2] Russian analyst Alexei Arbatov projects that Russian deployed strategic warhead numbers could fall even lower, perhaps to 1,000-1,100, leaving Moscow facing a decision on whether or not to build back up to 1,550.[3] In the spring of 2011, the Russian government reportedly decided to proceed with designing a new liquid-fueled heavy ICBM, which could offer the Russian military a cost-effective way to deploy a large number of warheads to reach the 1,550 level.

By contrast, the U.S. military will be able to sustain a force of 1,550 deployed strategic warheads on 700 deployed strategic delivery vehicles for the duration of New START. The Pentagon announced its planned force structure in 2010: 1,550 deployed strategic warheads on 240 deployed Trident D-5 SLBMs, 400 deployed Minuteman ICBMs, 40 deployed nuclear-capable bombers, and 20 additional deployed ICBMs or bombers.[4]

When signing New START in 2010, Obama called for another round of arms reduction negotiations, this one to include nonstrategic nuclear weapons and nondeployed strategic warheads. The United States reportedly has 500 nonstrategic nuclear warheads in its inventory, assuming that the 260 W80 warheads for sea-launched cruise missiles have now been retired and are in the queue for dismantlement. The U.S. nonstrategic nuclear inventory includes some 200 B61 bombs deployed in Europe.[5] The Russian nonstrategic nuclear arsenal in 2011 was believed to consist of 3,700-5,400 nuclear warheads of various types, including those for use on cruise missiles, tactical aircraft, and air defense systems. Many of these warheads were old and believed ready for retirement soon; the "nominal load" of Russian nonstrategic delivery systems was estimated to be 2,080 nonstrategic warheads.[6] (See Figure 2-2.)

	U.S.	Russia
Air-Delivered	500	800
Anti-Ballistic Missile/Air Defense	0	700
Ground-Based	0	?
Naval	0	600
Total	500	~2,100[7]

Figure 2-2. U.S. and Russian Non-Strategic Nuclear Weapons.[8]

WHAT THE RUSSIANS SAY

Medvedev and Obama committed to a step-by-step process of reducing nuclear arms in their April 1, 2009, joint statement at their initial meeting in London, England. The New START preamble notes the sides "seeking to preserve continuity in, and provide new impetus to, the step-by-step process of reducing and limiting nuclear arms." Medvedev, like Obama, has endorsed the goal of a world free of nuclear arms.

That said, Moscow has shown little enthusiasm for an early round of new nuclear arms reduction negotiations. Speaking at the United Nations (UN) Conference on Disarmament on March 1, 2011, Foreign Minister Sergey Lavrov stated:

> We insist that there is a clear need to take into account the factors that negatively affect strategic stability, such as plans to place weapons in outer space, to develop non-nuclear armed strategic offensive weapons, as well as unilateral deployment of a global BMD [ballistic missile defense] system. Nor could we ignore the considerable imbalances in conventional arms, especially against the background of dangerous conflicts persisting in many regions of the world.[9]

This reiterated a standard Russian line: issues which must be addressed in conjunction with, if not prior to, further nuclear arms reductions include missile defense, long-range conventional strike weapons, the fate of the CFE Treaty, and weapons in outer space. The mass of linkages that the Russians have insisted on—and adding that they appear reluctant to agree to cooperate on missile defense and have shown little creativity on the question of limiting conventional forces in Europe — makes for a daunting knot of issues. This may well reflect broader uncertainty or indecision in Moscow on where to go next on arms control with the United States.

As of the autumn of 2011, the Russian government had not articulated its thinking on what further reductions of strategic nuclear forces might entail and had said little about nonstrategic nuclear weapons. In his Conference on Disarmament speech, Lavrov indicated that withdrawal of nonstrategic nuclear weapons to the national territory of the state owning the weapons — U.S. nonstrategic B61 bombs deployed in Europe are the only weapons in this category — should be the first step in addressing nonstrategic nuclear arms. Lavrov and other Russians suggested that such withdrawal would be a precondition for negotiations on nonstrategic weapons.[10] Transparency regarding nonstrategic nuclear weapons might be a first step, but Moscow has not addressed this publicly.[11]

Unofficial Russian experts have offered ideas for addressing nonstrategic nuclear weapons, but they tend to shy away from proposing to limit the weapons directly. They instead suggested that the warheads could be "demated" (separated) from their delivery systems — most, if not all, Russian nonstrategic warheads already are demated from their delivery systems — and stored in "central" storage facilities located away from bases where the delivery systems are deployed. The storage facilities could be monitored to ensure that the warheads were not moved out and/or to confirm the number of warheads they contain, but not as pertaining to a direct numerical limit on the warheads. Inspections might also be conducted at former storage sites to confirm the absence of nuclear weapons.[12]

Russian officials also said that, before pursuing further nuclear cuts, Moscow wanted to observe how the New START Treaty was implemented.[13] Moreover, at that time, both countries faced presidential elections. With the September 24, 2011, announcement that Vladimir Putin would run in the March 2012 election for the presidency (with Medvedev to become prime minister), it was a virtual certainty that Putin would assume the office in May, and indeed he did. As Putin has undoubtedly been involved in all major foreign as well as domestic policy decisions during his tenure as prime minister, his return to the presidency should not mean a major shift in Russian arms control policy. He has, however, a more skeptical view of the United States than does Medvedev. The Russian bureaucracy, moreover, is unlikely to show much daring or creativity.

Moscow is also watching the 2012 U.S. presidential election. Consequently, the Russian government may wait until it sees the outcome of the election in November 2012 before deciding how to proceed on further nuclear arms cuts.[14] The Russians also believe that the Obama administration will be cautious about arms control steps, fearing that such steps could become politicized as the U.S. election campaign heats up.[15]

CONVENTIONAL WEAKNESS AND NUCLEAR DEPENDENCE

Russian conventional force capabilities have declined dramatically since the collapse of the Soviet Union. Large numbers of tanks, armored personnel carriers, artillery, tactical aircraft, and helicopters were located on the territories of non-Russian republics, and most of that equipment ended up as part of the militaries of those states. In addition, the Russian military budget suffered greatly during the economic downturn of the 1990s. This led to striking changes. For example, while NATO long worried about the Soviet numerical advantage in main battle tanks, in 2009 NATO had a more than 2:1 advantage over Russia in tanks in the CFE Treaty area of application.[16] NATO likewise leads in other key categories of conventional military equipment where it long lagged behind the Soviet Union and Warsaw Pact (this, in part, reflects the fact that most former members of the Warsaw Pact have since joined NATO).

Moscow has announced a major conventional rearmament plan, with the goal that 70 percent of the military's weapons and equipment should be modernized by 2020. It remains unclear how much real capability this will add. The plan called for some $700 billion in new arms procurement over the decade to 2020 but faces major challenges. Corruption in the defense sector has traditionally siphoned sizable funds away from their stated purposes. It is not clear that the Russian defense industry will be able to meet the demands for modern military equipment, particularly in the high-tech sector.[17] In June 2011, Russia concluded a contract with France for the purchase of two *Mistral* class helicopter assault ships (and the option to build two more in Russia). In July 2011 Medvedev expressed concern about the quality and cost of Russian-produced military equipment, suggesting to Defense Minister Anatoliy Serdyukov that he consider purchasing other equipment from foreign sources.[18]

Russian analysts also worried that Russia would be unable to compete with other militaries in high-tech areas. Take tactical air power, for example: Russia has only begun flight-testing a 5th generation fighter, while the U.S. military has already completed its purchase of the F-22 and will shortly begin receiving the F-35. Moreover, Russia has nothing to compare to the unmanned drone aircraft that already provide the U.S. air force with major reconnaissance, surveillance, and strike assets.

Russian analysts expressed particular concern about U.S. long-range, precision-guided conventional strike weapons, such as conventionally-armed sea- and air-launched cruise missiles, for which the Russian military had no real counterpart. Some suggested that the United States could use long-range, precision-guided conventional weapons to strike targets that previously would have required nuclear weapons, such as silo-based ICBMs. Arbatov wrote that the United States might deploy as many as 3,000-5,000 long-range, conventionally-armed cruise missiles, though he noted that preparations for a major conventional counterforce campaign would take time and would be visible.[19] A senior Russian foreign ministry official downplayed this concern, noting that Russia would respond — and the United States should understand that Russia would respond — with strategic nuclear weapons to a large-scale U.S. effort to degrade Russian strategic nuclear forces with conventional strike systems.[20] (It is also unclear whether there is a solid basis for Arbatov's concern; senior U.S. Air Force officers discount the ability of conventionally-armed cruise missile warheads to disable hardened ICBM silos.[21])

In any event, the Russian military in 2011 lacked a clear picture of when it might have large numbers of conventional strike weapons of its own. Above and beyond the question of equipment, the Russian military faces a shrinking and less well-trained manpower base. Due to demographic trends, the number of Russian males eligible for the draft in 2017 will be about half the number in 2006, and it is already difficult to find a sufficient number of healthy draftees.[22] The conscription period has been slashed over the past decade from 2 years to 1, and the military leadership continues to be aloof to the notion of an all- or mostly all-professional force.

Medvedev and Serdyukov launched the latest in Russia's post-Soviet military reforms in the autumn of 2008. The reform path—which has included downsizing the military, particularly the officer corps; reorganizing the army into a brigade-based system; and raising the alert status of all units—has made some progress, but it has not been steady. After announcing that the officer corps would be downsized by 205,000, which would bring the number of officers down to 150,000, in early 2011, the defense ministry raised the new total of outgoing officers to 220,000. It is unclear how much progress the army has made in adopting the brigade system.[23]

Weaknesses in Russian conventional forces—and the uncertain prospects for military modernization and reform over the coming decade—mean that nuclear weapons will likely remain central to Russian military strategy for the foreseeable future. A number of Russian analysts have expressed concern about conventional force imbalances and their potential impact on strategic nuclear stability. For example, Andrei Kokoshin noted the increase in U.S. conventional capabilities and wrote that "nuclear weapons act as a sort of equalizer . . . and we still do not see any credible signs that the West is ready to eliminate the imbalance in general-purpose forces and conventional weapons."[24]

For its part, the new Russian military doctrine issued in early 2010 stated that:

> The Russian Federation reserves the right to utilize nuclear weapons in response to the utilization of nuclear and other types of weapons of mass destruction against it and (or) its allies, and also in the event of aggression against the Russian Federation involving the use of conventional weapons when the very existence of the state is under threat.[25]

The doctrine appeared to narrow somewhat the circumstances in which nuclear weapons might be used compared to its 2000 predecessor, but it offered few specifics about the roles of strategic or nonstrategic nuclear weapons. Indeed, it did not draw a distinction between strategic and nonstrategic nuclear arms.

Conventional disadvantages appear to explain much of the Russian attachment to nonstrategic nuclear weapons. Although the Russian government appears reluctant to speak publicly of a Chinese military threat or challenge, the Russian military may see little alternative to nuclear weapons for dealing with a large Chinese army equipped with increasingly modern conventional arms. That said, the logic for maintaining so many nonstrategic nuclear warheads is not clear; how many such nuclear weapons would the Russian military employ against an invading Chinese force before the conflict escalated to strategic nuclear strikes against the homeland? The number is certainly well below the thousands of weapons currently in the Russian nonstrategic nuclear arsenal.

MISSILE DEFENSE

On the 2011 arms control agenda, Moscow (as well as Washington) attached the greatest priority to the issue of missile defense and the possibility of missile defense cooperation. Russian concerns focused on the "phased adaptive approach" based on the Standard SM-3 missile interceptor; the Russians expressed little concern about the 30 ground-based interceptors deployed at Fort Greely, Alaska and Vandenberg Air Force Base, California.

Under the phased adaptive approach, SM-3 Bloc IA missiles were deployed on board ships in the Mediterranean Sea in Phase 1 (the *Aegis*-class cruiser *Monterrey* made the first Mediterranean deployment in the spring of 2011). Bloc IB missiles with upgraded seekers will be deployed ashore in Romania in 2015 in Phase 2; Bloc IIA missiles with higher velocities will be deployed in Poland in 2018 in Phase 3; and Bloc IIB missiles with still higher velocities will be deployed in 2020 in Phase 4. Although some Russian analysts expressed concern about Phase 3; most focused on Phase 4, when the SM-3 Bloc IIB missile is to be given some capability to intercept ICBMs.

U.S. officials do not believe the planned missile defense system poses a serious threat to Russian strategic ballistic missile forces. Bloc IIB would constitute only a portion of the total planned buy of 450-550 SM-3 interceptors, and its deployment in Poland and Romania would mean that it would not be well-positioned to intercept Russian ICBMs headed across the Arctic.[26] U.S. defense department officials have reportedly made this point, with accompanying technical presentations, to their Russian counterparts.

In 2011, Russian officials professed not to be persuaded. Some voiced concern about scenarios that appeared highly unlikely, e.g., the deployment of most or all SM-3 equipped warships into the Arctic Ocean to defend the United States against Russian ICBMs. Much Russian concern may be related to what comes after 2020 should U.S. missile defense continue to progress. Finally, some Russian concern was politically-motivated: Moscow is not happy about the prospect of *any* U.S. military hardware deployed in Poland and Romania.

In discussions with their U.S. counterparts, Russian officials sought a legally-binding guarantee that U.S. and Russian missile defense systems would not be directed against the other side's strategic forces. They have also sought agreement on criteria regarding parameters such as the number, velocity, and location of missile defense interceptors (the criteria are sometimes described as being reminiscent of those in the 1997 ABM Treaty demarcation agreement that was intended to distinguish theater missile defense interceptors from ABM interceptors).

The U.S. Government stressed its readiness to be transparent about U.S. missile defense plans and capabilities; the head of the U.S. Missile Defense Agency offered to allow the Russians to monitor SM-3 tests so that they could be assured that the interceptors lacked the range and velocity to engage ICBMs. Washington was also prepared to offer political assurances at the highest level that its planned system was not directed against Russian missiles. U.S. policy is to defend the United States against *limited* ballistic missile attacks, such as might be mounted in the future by North Korea or Iran, not a Russian missile attack. Washington balked, however, at a legally-binding guarantee and at criteria that appear to resemble limits; neither would be ratifiable by the Senate.

U.S. and Russian officials had hoped to have a joint statement of principles for missile defense cooperation for release by the presidents at their May 2011 meeting in Deauville, France, but the sides failed to reach final agreement on the language. Missile defense was discussed further at the June NATO-Russia defense ministers' meeting and during Lavrov's mid-July visit to Washington. No significant progress was reported from these meetings, but U.S., NATO, and Russian officials seemed to take care to leave the door open. For example, in a November 23 statement that appeared aimed largely at the Russian domestic audience, Medvedev sharply criticized U.S. missile defense plans and threatened Russian countermeasures; he made clear, however, that Russia remained open to discussions with the United States and NATO. Despite the appearance of an impasse at the end of the year, U.S. officials continued to pursue the dialogue with their Russian counterparts.

While Washington and Moscow disagree on a legally-binding guarantee (as opposed to political assurances) and criteria, the sides' positions reportedly converged on what practical missile defense cooperation might include: a U.S.-Russia defense technical cooperation agreement that would enable exchange of sensitive information; NATO-Russia theater missile defense exercises; a joint NATO-Russia data fusion center as a venue to exchange early warning data from the sides' radars and other sensors; and a NATO-Russia planning and operations center to develop ideas for further cooperation. U.S. and Russian officials also discussed, though made less progress on, the idea of a joint analysis of the impact of missile defense on strategic deterrence.[27]

U.S. officials argued that Russia should set aside its demands for legally-binding guarantees and criteria and engage in practical cooperation, which would give Moscow significant insights into the U.S. missile defense system. If that did not allay Russian concerns, Moscow would always be free later to withdraw from a cooperative plan. Public Russian pronouncements in 2011 suggested that Moscow was not then prepared to accept that approach.

It is not clear what the Russians want on missile defense or why they are so reluctant about missile defense cooperation; some may fear that agreement to cooperation with the United States and NATO would "bless" the planned U.S. missile defense deployments in Europe. However, the Russian government presumably understands that, with NATO having adopted the territorial defense mission at its 2010 Lisbon, Portugal, summit, it would be difficult for Moscow to sow division among allies on this issue; missile defense will not prove to be a controversial issue like medium-range missiles were in the 1980s. It may be that Moscow has not made up its mind about how to handle missile defense.

This creates another problem. The Russians repeatedly said that they should be in on the ground floor of any effort to define a cooperative missile defense arrangement for Europe, but U.S. and NATO plans moved forward regardless. For example, in September 2011, it was announced that the United States would base four *Aegis*-class warships in Rota, Spain, and that an AN/TPY-2 radar would be deployed in Turkey, as the United States and NATO proceeded with implementation of the phased adaptive approach. The longer the Russians wait to agree to missile defense cooperation, the less influence they may have on the architecture that emerges.

FURTHER NUCLEAR WEAPONS REDUCTIONS

As noted earlier, Russian officials have stipulated a number of issues that they say should be addressed in conjunction with, or prior to, further negotiations on reducing nuclear arms. Nevertheless, there are several factors that might motivate Moscow to consider further negotiations, even if they did not achieve full satisfaction on their other issues.

First, Russian strategic nuclear forces have declined to a number very close to the New START limit of 1,550 deployed strategic warheads and have fallen well below the limit of 700 deployed strategic delivery vehicles. Most analysts expect Russian strategic force levels to decline further, as older systems are retired faster than new systems can be deployed. Should the number drop to 1,000, as Arbatov wrote is possible, there would be a significant gap between Russian and U.S. numbers. The U.S. military can—and intends to—sustain a force of 1,550 deployed strategic warheads and 700 deployed strategic delivery vehicles. (See Figure 2-3.)

	U.S.[28]	Russia[29]
Deployed ICBMs	420	192
Warheads on deployed ICBMs	420	542
Deployed SLBMs	240	128
Warheads on deployed SLBMs	1,090	640
Deployed heavy bombers	40	76
Warheads attributed to deployed heavy bombers	40	76
Total deployed ICBMs, SLBMs, heavy bombers	700	396
Total warheads attributed	1,550	1,258

Figure 2-3. Notional U.S. and Russian Strategic Offensive Forces Under New START.

One way to close this gap without a major Russian buildup would be a new agreement that reduced the limit on deployed strategic warheads, perhaps to 1,000. It would appear that Russia could sustain a force of that level with its current SLBM, Topol-M, and Yars ICBM plans. It might not have to develop and deploy a new heavy ICBM, which would be costly and potentially destabilizing, in that it would result in many Russian warheads on a relatively small number of fixed aim points and raise concern in the United States about silo-based Minuteman survivability.

A second reason that the Russians might engage in further negotiations is to secure limits on nondeployed strategic warheads or otherwise reduce U.S. "upload" potential (the ability to put additional warheads on existing ICBMs and SLBMs). The United States will implement much of its New START reductions by "downloading" missiles, that is, by removing one or more warheads but keeping the missile deployed. The Department of Defense (DoD) stated in 2010 that, under New START, all Minuteman III ICBMs — each of which can carry three warheads — will be downloaded to carry a single warhead. Trident D-5 SLBMs — each of which can carry eight warheads — will also be significantly downloaded, so that they will carry an average of four-five warheads.

At least initially, downloaded U.S. warheads will go into storage (there is already a long queue of nuclear warheads awaiting dismantlement). It would not be difficult to upload, or return, them to ICBMs and SLBMs, were the New START Treaty to break down. It appears that the United States will have the capacity to upload warheads and increase the number of its deployed strategic warheads on ICBMs and SLBMs to 2,650-2,850.

The Russians do not have a comparable ability. Russia is expected to implement its New START reductions by eliminating missiles, with the residual missiles carrying full or close to full warhead sets. Thus, even if Russia has additional ballistic missile warheads, it will have no spaces on ballistic missiles on which to put them. A new negotiation could produce direct limits on nondeployed strategic warheads, reducing the American advantage in upload potential.

Some Russian experts have suggested that Moscow could deal with the upload problem by reducing the limit on deployed strategic delivery vehicles to below the New START level of 700. That would reduce the number of spaces into which extra warheads might be uploaded but, as long as the United States has some downloaded missiles, it would retain some upload capability.

A third reason why Russia might be interested in further negotiations is to secure the permanent removal of U.S. nonstrategic nuclear weapons from Europe, something that Moscow has long sought. Washington is unlikely to accept this as a precondition for negotiations on nonstrategic nuclear arms, but U.S. officials privately indicated that it could be an outcome of a negotiation, depending on the other terms of the agreement.[30]

U.S. nonstrategic nuclear weapons in Europe probably represent a relatively small bargaining chip. Moscow analysts undoubtedly noted that a number of NATO member states have expressed interest in a reduction in or complete withdrawal of those weapons. This was not a unanimous Alliance view; other allies believe that a U.S. nuclear presence should remain. But those states favoring removal of U.S. weapons included Germany, the Netherlands, and Belgium, on whose territory U.S. nuclear weapons reportedly are stored, and whose decisions on modernizing—or not modernizing—dual-capable aircraft might make those weapons' continued presence on their territory superfluous.

Taken together, these factors would appear to give the Russians reasons to seek a round of negotiations on further reductions, although Moscow was not prepared for negotiations in 2011 and may choose to wait until after the outcome of the 2012 U.S. presidential election is known. As 2011 drew to a close, U.S. officials appeared to accept that comprehensive negotiations might have to wait until 2013, but they thought there was a possibility that bilateral consultations on nuclear arms reductions might get underway before then.

If/when Russia agrees to a further negotiation, it will be a more difficult and drawn-out process than the negotiation that produced New START in less than 1 year. The sides will negotiate more carefully as numbers go down. Bringing nondeployed strategic warheads and nonstrategic nuclear weapons into the negotiations, assuming that the Russians agree, will introduce challenging new questions, such as how to limit and monitor limits on warheads in storage areas. It will not be an 11-month negotiation, as was the process that produced New START.

Finally, Moscow likely will not be prepared for truly radical cuts in a next round of negotiations. There is some level of deployed strategic warheads—and/or total nuclear warheads—below which the Russians will not reduce without addressing third-country forces, at least those of Britain, France, and China. (Washington likely has a level of its own; given the range of other U.S. military capabilities, that level probably is lower than the Russian level.) Some Russian analysts have previously suggested that Russia would not be prepared to reduce to below 1,000 deployed strategic warheads without bringing in third countries and perhaps applying limits on missile defense.

CONVENTIONAL WEAPONS AND FORCES

The Russians have not yet proposed a way to address their concerns about long-range conventional strike weapons. Should conventional warheads be placed on ICBMs or SLBMs, they would be captured under the New START limit on deployed strategic warheads. In essence, the United States would have to give up one nuclear warhead for each conventional warhead it deployed on a strategic ballistic missile. In any case, U.S. officials have stated that they do not intend to place conventional warheads on ICBMs or SLBMs. The Pentagon, however, is developing a hypersonic glide vehicle, which could rapidly strike targets at intercontinental distances. U.S. officials have argued that such a vehicle would not be captured by the definitions and limits of New START. However, should the United States proceed with development of that vehicle, the Russians will undoubtedly raise it as an issue in New START's Bilateral Consultative Commission.

Moscow has expressed concern about other types of conventional strike weapons, such as long-range cruise missiles. It is difficult to see the United States accepting constraints on such weapons, which are key to U.S. conventional power projection. U.S. military officials do not see conventionally-armed cruise missiles as posing a threat to Russian strategic targets; they do not believe the warheads are large enough to disable ICBM silos. A military-to-military dialogue might explore whether the threat is real or not, but it is not clear whether that could by itself assuage Russian concerns.

The other conventional issue is the fate of the CFE Treaty. Signed in 1991, the Treaty originally constrained NATO and Warsaw Pact holdings of key equipment, such as tanks, armored personnel carriers, artillery, attack helicopters, and tactical aircraft. The treaty was "adapted" in 1999 to reflect the end of the Warsaw Pact and apply national limits vice limits on NATO and Warsaw Pact holdings. Due to Russia's failure to live up to political commitments regarding its forces in Georgia and Moldova, NATO countries have not ratified the Adapted CFE Treaty (Moscow disputed this linkage). In 2007, Russia announced that it was suspending its observance of the original treaty, though it does not appear to have exceeded its overall CFE equipment entitlements.

Attempts have been made to revive the CFE regime. During the second George W. Bush term, U.S. officials proposed a "parallel actions" approach, under which NATO would move to ratify the Adapted CFE Treaty and take other steps, such as preparing to bring the Baltic States into the treaty, in parallel with Russia implementing its 1999 commitments. In 2010, U.S. officials attempted to define principles for reviving conventional arms control but could not find a formula with Russia that would work. One particularly difficult question proved to be host nation consent, i.e., a nation's right to determine the presence of foreign forces on its soil. U.S. and Russian officials failed to find a formulation to sidestep the issues of South Ossetia and Abkhazia, where Russian forces are stationed with the consent of local authorities but without Georgian consent.

Were the sides able to resolve the host nation consent question, the Russians would like to reduce the limits on equipment for NATO member states. As most, if not all, NATO members are below — in some cases, significantly below — their CFE entitlements, this might not pose a major problem. More difficult would be the flank question. Moscow strongly opposes flank limits that constrain where Russia deploys CFE-limited equipment on Russian territory. While the U.S. military attaches no importance to the flank limits, those restrictions matter to countries such as Georgia, Turkey, Norway, and the Baltic states. It is difficult to see a compromise on this question.

By 2011, U.S. officials had concluded that the CFE Treaty regime likely could not be saved. Moscow had not offered steps that might preserve the treaty and its limits or open the way for a mutually acceptable successor regime. On November 22, 2011, the Department of State announced that the United States would "cease carrying out certain obligations" to Russia related to data provision and acceptance of inspections. All other NATO states shortly thereafter followed suit. The Russians did not seem unduly alarmed; they may assume, perhaps correctly, that fiscal difficulties will mean reductions in the conventional forces of most NATO countries in any case.

While suspending its observance of the CFE Treaty's transparency and observation provisions, the Russians have continued to observe the requirements of the Vienna Document on Confidence- and Security-Building Measures (CSBMs) and the Open Skies Treaty. One possible way forward would be to set aside equipment limits for the time being and focus on expanding the Vienna Document CSBMs to include some of the transparency and observation provisions of the CFE Treaty. The negotiation would still have to deal with host nation consent, but it might be simpler in the context of CSBMs rather than limits. It is not clear how Moscow would respond to such an approach.

CONCLUSION

There is a full arms control agenda between the United States (and NATO), on the one hand, and Russia, on the other. Whether progress is possible depends in large part on decisions that Moscow may not yet have taken. The impending U.S. presidential election, moreover, complicates prospects for arms control negotiations in 2012. In the near term, prospects appear limited to the (apparently declining) possibility of an agreement on a cooperative missile defense system for Europe, transparency measures regarding non-strategic nuclear weapons, and consultations on arms control issues. While Moscow may have incentives in the medium term to negotiate on further nuclear arms reductions, more formal negotiations and more meaningful proposals will have to wait until 2013.

ENDNOTES - CHAPTER 2

1. U.S. Department of State, Fact Sheet, "New START Treaty Aggregate Numbers of Strategic Offensive Arms," October 25, 2011, available from *www.state.gov/documents/organization/176308. pdf.* This table uses New START counting rules, which count the actual number of warheads on deployed intercontinental ballistic missiles (ICBMs) and sea-launched ballistic missiles (SLBMs) plus one warhead for each deployed nuclear-capable bomber (even though bombers can carry more than one weapon).

2. Pavel Podvig projects a Russian strategic force of 396 deployed strategic delivery vehicles and 1,258 deployed strategic

warheads. See Pavel Podvig, "New START Treaty in Numbers," *Russian Strategic Nuclear Forces*, available from *russianforces.org/ blog/2010/03/new_start_treaty_in_numbers.shtml*. Hans Kristensen projects slightly higher levels: 403 deployed strategic delivery vehicles and 1,349 deployed strategic warheads; private exchange with the author, July 2010. Some Pentagon officials question whether Russia will go so low, noting that Russian negotiators in New Strategic Arms Reduction Treaty (New START) held out for a limit of 1,550 deployed strategic warheads rather than the U.S. proposal of 1,500, though Russian resistance to 1,500 could have been due to Moscow's reluctance to accept the opening U.S. proposal.

3. Alexei Arbatov, "Gambit or Endgame? The New State of Arms Control," Moscow, Russia: Carnegie Moscow Center, March 2011, p. 14.

4. The Pentagon has yet to say whether its force will include 400 ICBMs and 60 bombers or 420 ICBMs and 40 bombers. Since the Air Force plans to deploy only single-warhead ICBMs and New START counts each bomber as one warhead, the decision will not affect the deployed strategic warhead count.

5. Exchange with Hans Kristensen, June 2011.

6. Hans M. Kristensen and Robert Norris, "Russian Nuclear Forces, 2011," *Bulletin of the Atomic Scientists*, Vol. 67, No. 3, May 2011, pp. 71-73.

7. This is the "nominal load" of warheads that could be carried by Russian nonstrategic delivery systems; the total Russian nonstrategic nuclear inventory is believed to be in the range of 3,700-5,400 warheads.

8. "Russian Nuclear Forces, 2011." Note that it is unclear whether or not there is a nuclear warhead for the Russian Iskandr ground-based surface-to-surface missile.

9. Ministry of Foreign Affairs of the Russian Federation, Information and Press Department, "Statement by H.E. Mr. Sergey Lavrov, Minister of Foreign Affairs of the Russian Federation, at the Plenary meeting of the Conference on Disarmament, Geneva, Switzerland, March 1, 2011," available from *www.ln.mid.ru/*

bdomp/brp_4.nsf/e78a48070f128a7b43256999005bcbb3/2de66a92e764 dbb8c3257846004dfd44!OpenDocument.

10. Some Russian statements go further, suggesting that the withdrawal of U.S. nuclear weapons from Europe must be accompanied by elimination of any nuclear infrastructure on the territory of European members of the North Atlantic Treaty Oganization (NATO) and an end to NATO nuclear exercises.

11. Conversation with senior Russian foreign ministry official, May 2011.

12. See, for example, "Gambit or Endgame," pp. 31-33; and Anatoliy S. Diakov, "Verified Reductions in Non-Strategic Nuclear Weapons," Moscow, Russia: Center for Arms Control, Energy and Environmental Studies, Moscow Institute for Physics and Technology, February 18, 2011, available from *www.armscontrol.ru/.*

13. See, for example, "Russia Says Too Early to Talk about Tactical Nuclear Weapons with United States," *RIA Novosti,* January 29, 2011, available from *en.rian.ru/mlitary_news/20110129/162362622. html.*

14. Conversation with senior Russian foreign ministry official, May 2011.

15. Conversation with senior Russian diplomat, August 2011.

16. In 2007, Russia's last data declaration before it suspended its observance of the Conventional Forces in Europe (CFE) Treaty reported 5,063 main battle tanks. NATO's January 2009 data declaration reported 12,486. See Dorn Crawford, "Conventional Armed Forces in Europe (CFE): A Review and Update of Key Treaty Elements," U.S. Department of State, March 2009.

17. See Roger N. McDermott, "Russia's Conventional Military Weakness and Substrategic Nuclear Policy," Fort Leavenworth, KS: The Foreign Military Studies Office, pp. 19-22, for a more detailed discussion of the Russian military's 10-year procurement plan and the challenges that it faces.

18. Anatoly Medetsky, "Medvedev Threatens to Start Importing Arms," *Moscow Times,* July 13, 2011, available from *www.themoscowtimes.com/news/article/medvedev-threatens-to-start-importing-arms/440428.html.*

19. "Gambit or Endgame?," pp. 19-23.

20. Conversation with senior Russian foreign ministry official, May 2011.

21. Conversation with U.S. Strategic Command officers, August 2010.

22. Keir Giles, "Where Have All the Soldiers Gone? Russia's Military Plans versus Demographic Reality," Shrivenham, UK: Conflict Studies Research Centre, Defence Academy of the United Kingdom, October 2006, p. 2.

23. See "Russia's Conventional Military Weakness and Sub-strategic Nuclear Policy," pp. 14-17, for a discussion of the ups and downs of the Russian military's latest reform effort.

24. Andrei Kokoshin, "Ensuring Strategic Stability in the Past and Present: Theoretical and Applied Questions," Cambridge, MA: Harvard Kennedy School, Belfer Center for Science and International Affairs, 2011, p. 57.

25. "The Military Doctrine of the Russian Federation," approved by Russian Presidential Edict on February 5, 2010.

26. It is expected that the SM-3 Bloc IIB will be liquid-fueled in order to achieve the desired velocity to engage ICBMs; that may mean that Bloc IIB interceptors are deployed only onshore, as the U.S. navy traditionally prefers solid-fueled missiles for fire safety reasons.

27. Conversations with U.S. Government officials, July 2011.

28. This column assumes that the United States chooses to keep 420 deployed Minuteman III ICBMs, which will require that deployed U.S. nuclear-capable bombers be reduced to 40. If the

Department of Defense (DoD) were to choose to keep more than 40 bombers (it has said it may keep up to 60), it would have to reduce one deployed Minuteman III for each bomber over 40.

29. This column is based on calculations by Pavel Podvig, "New START Treaty in Numbers," Russian Strategic Nuclear Forces, available from *russianforces.org/blog/2010/03/new_start_treaty_in_numbers.shtml*. A different calculation provided to the author by Hans M. Kristensen in July 2010 projected a total of 403 Russian deployed ICBMs, SLBMs, and heavy bombers attributed with 1,349 warheads under New START. Some DoD officials question whether the Russians would reduce their deployed strategic weapons so low, noting that the Russians originally proposed a strategic warhead limit of 1,675 and did not accept the U.S.-proposed limit of 1,500, agreeing in the end to a limit of 1,550. The Russian government has not publicly described its intended strategic force structure under New START, and the U.S. Government has not produced an unclassified estimate of that structure.

30. U.S. views on this will likely be affected by the views of NATO allies. Some allies feel strongly that a U.S. nuclear presence should remain in Europe; whether or not they would be comfortable with the removal of those weapons would depend in part on the nature of the reductions taken on the Russian side and on other steps that NATO might take to assure them of the Alliance's commitment to their security.

CHAPTER 3

RUSSIAN VIEWS ON NUCLEAR WEAPONS AND GLOBAL ZERO: IMPLICATIONS AND CONSEQUENCES

Peter R. Huessy

Russia sees "Global Zero" — the effort to move the world's nuclear powers to eliminate all their nuclear weapons — as a means for the United States to enhance the effectiveness of its own conventional capability. Ironically, U.S. analysts have echoed this, claiming that Global Zero, which they support, "would make it easier for the U.S. to defend allies and interests overseas."[1]

In addition, while advocates of U.S. movement toward zero nuclear weapons often speak of the immorality of the United States maintaining thousands of nuclear weapons both deployed and stockpiled, the Russians do not see moral delinquency or hypocrisy in their own maintenance of 5,000 or more tactical or strategic nuclear weapons.

Given this difference in views, it is highly uncertain whether the U.S. pursuit of more nuclear arms control beyond the New Strategic Arms Reduction Treaty (New START) will strengthen U.S. efforts to "isolate Iran" with Russian help. Russia feels no pressure to reduce its nuclear weaponry and is in no rush to see U.S. conventional superiority dominate geostrategic relations.

RUSSIAN VIEWS ON NUCLEAR TECHNOLOGY

Russian views on specific nuclear weapons technology also parallel their views on the deployment of such weapons. Major U.S. efforts have been made for the past 30 years to make the strategic balance more stable as both the United States and the Union of Soviet Socialist Republics (USSR) (and now Russia) have pursued major reductions in nuclear weapons. One of the central tenets of the second Strategic Arms Reduction Treaty (START II) was the elimination of multiple warhead land-based missiles.

As nuclear weapons platforms, (bombers, submarines, and land-based silo-deployed missiles) are reduced in number, the worry was that too few numbers would encourage an attack during a crisis, because an adversary could see the possibility of eliminating our ability to retaliate after suffering an initial attack. So there were efforts to reduce warheads while keeping the number of "platforms" as high as possible.

Russian strategic thought has long seen U.S. deployments as threatening, especially missile defenses, but Russian development of new nuclear weapons is universally described by Moscow as "intended to trump" other similar missiles of other nuclear powers.[2] Russia apparently sees little "destabilizing" in the deployment of missiles capable of carrying a heavily multiple independent reentry vehicled (MIRVed) contingent of warheads. Such weapons are a significant portion of its inventory and will probably increase as Russia seeks to maintain the deployment of 1,550 warheads allowed by new START but with fewer overall platforms.

RUSSIAN VIEWS OF THE UTILITY OF NUCLEAR WEAPONS

There is also the factor that the Russians see nuclear weapons as actually "increasing" in utility as their own conventional capability declines, as opposed to a near universal assumption among Global Zero advocates that nuclear weapons have very little actual utility in today's geostrategic environment. Russia sees nuclear weapons as a key capability to offset its conventional inferiority in the European theater and in their near abroad. It sees nuclear weapons as a leveler in its relations with China, as its military analysts have repeatedly raised concerns over hegemonic Chinese ambitions in East Asia.

Moscow also sees nuclear weapons as a means of practicing peacetime coercion. They have reputedly threatened the use of nuclear weapons against eastern European and Baltic states to counter cooperative missile defense efforts with the United States. According to some Russian commentary, nuclear weapons are needed to reverse the prospects of a major conventional defeat. As one top U.S. analyst told me, in Russia's view, "Nukes on big rockets with lots of room for error makes lots of sense." He concluded our conversation by noting that nuclear weapons allow the Russians to "reign in hell rather than serve in Heaven."[3]

DOES CONVENTIONAL WISDOM REFLECT ACTUAL RUSSIAN NUCLEAR POLICY?

Alexei Arbatov, in his March 2011 Carnegie Paper on Russian nuclear weapons policy, concluded that Russia maintains a conservative, not reckless, nuclear policy, and will not even be able to deploy up to New START ceilings While interested in even further reductions in nuclear weapons, Russia would find that such cuts would be impossible because of U.S. deployments of ballistic missile defenses, development of new long-range prompt strike, and existing tactical nuclear weapons. Arbtov goes even further with the claim that Moscow has to rely on tactical nuclear weapons as a counterbalance not only to North Atlantic Treaty Organization (NATO) conventional superiority[4] but also to U.S. strategic nuclear superiority and long-range precision-guided weapons.

This "wisdom" has led such members of Congress as Barney Frank and Edward Markey to propose radical and unilateral reductions in U.S. nuclear forces, as well as elimination of the entire modernization and sustainment funding for the entire U.S. nuclear enterprise. Frank[5] has pushed further cuts in U.S. defense spending of $1 trillion, including nuclear forces, to a point where the United States would be left with 160 Minuteman missiles (from the 450 deployed today), seven *Trident* submarines (from the currently deployed 12), and no strategic bombers. Moreover, Frank calls for no modernization funding, nor does Markey. In fact, Markey claims the United States is currently spending some $70 billion a year on nuclear weapons and "related" programs, thus justifying a cut of $20 billion annually as being only a small price to pay to further reduce U.S. spending. But this is utter nonsense, of course.

According to the "Section 1251" report[6] submitted to the U.S. Senate prior to the final debate on the ratification of the New START treaty, the administration pledged that a total of roughly $215 billion would be spent over a period of 10 years to "sustain and modernize" the U.S. strategic nuclear deterrents, including the launch platforms on which our warheads are deployed, the national laboratories where the sustainment work on the warheads is done, and the stockpile stewardship activities.

Cutting $20 billion from these programs would essentially eliminate all U.S. nuclear sustainment and modernization. Such a draconian step is consistent with Markey's call for a "nuclear freeze," an echo of the Soviet-led nuclear freeze campaign of some 30 years ago initiated in response to the election of President Ronald Reagan and the initiation of the U.S. strategic modernization effort outlined in the Scowcroft Commission report of March 1983.

CONCLUSIONS: TRUTHS AND CONSEQUENCES

We have emphasized in the arms control narrative that further agreements with Russia on nuclear weapons reductions can be used as leverage by Moscow to curtail a host of U.S. defense requirements and capabilities, including prompt global conventional strike, missile defenses, and U.S. and allied conventional capabilities.[7] That idea has now morphed into an effort within Congress to bring to a halt all further nuclear modernization, despite current major Russian nuclear modernization.

Ironically, even as Moscow threatens to use its significant advantage in tactical nuclear weapons for coercion and blackmail in such areas as the geopolitical game over the Caspian basin energy resources, the competition to control the flow of oil to China, and NATO missile defense deployments, pressure grows in the United States to restrain the very U.S. and allied military deployments that could guard against such Russian adventures.

Even more worrisome, instead of seeking Russian restraint in its own nuclear weapons policy, especially its relatively cavalier attitude toward the use of nuclear weapons, we have tended to look the other way on Russian (and Chinese) contributions to nuclear proliferation elsewhere especially with regard to Iran, Syria, Venezuela, and North Korea, which they see keeping in check American power and influence as part of their zero-sum security policy perspective.

Understandably, because of the very large tactical nuclear weapons advantage of Russia, we have made it a central subject of future negotiations with Russia. Russia thus knows it can exact heavy concessions in exchange for its promise of movement on tactical nuclear weapons. Moreover, it can expect considerable restraint from the United States, as Washington promises itself that its own restraint will engender the proper response from Moscow.[8]

We have to remember that Russia begins with an attachment to nuclear weapons to guarantee its seat at the world power table. The more we grant Moscow leverage over an entire range of U.S. military deployments, the more we are cementing current Russian policy long into the future.[9]

SUMMARY

Many domestic analysts have called for major U.S. restraint in: (1) deployment of its conventional forces in Europe and the Far East; (2) deployment of prompt global conventional strike capabilities; (3) acceptance of major restrictions on the geographic location and number of deployed missile defense interceptors; (4) elimination of U.S. upload capability on its strategic nuclear force structure; and finally (5) overall serious restriction of U.S. space programs to avoid what is popularly termed "the weaponization of space."

U.S. restraint is needed, so the conventional wisdom goes, primarily to secure Russian cooperation on another "arms control deal," but also to further a policy Reset with Moscow which will enable a more cooperative relationship to emerge that helps with key counterproliferation problems with Iran and North Korea.

In fact, U.S. efforts have also enabled the Russians to gain important leverage over U.S. security policy without having to change significantly their own security behavior, especially their actions on nuclear weapons technology, their declaration of the utility of nuclear weapons, and their continued support for state sponsors of terror such as Syria and Iran. In addition, U.S. assumptions that Russia shares administration support for Global Zero are seriously wrong, as Russia is using the U.S. pursuit of that lofty goal as a means of securing U.S. restraint in U.S. nuclear modernization and deployment of U.S. and allied missile defenses.

ENDNOTES - CHAPTER 3

1. Bruce Blair wrote in *Arms Control Today* that the United States must limit its continental United States missile defense interceptors to significantly less than even the 100 allowed by the now defunct Anti-Ballistic Missile (ABM) Treaty or the number now maintained by Moscow, probably no more than 30-40.

2. On August 10, 2011, Putin announced plans for a new sub-fired ballistic missile with capability of firing 6-12 warheads per missile.

3. A specially upgraded *Akula*-class submarine has been caught trying to record the acoustic signature made by the *Vanguard* submarines that carry Trident nuclear missiles, with Britain recording the highest number of contacts with Russian submarines since 1987 according to the *London Telegraph* dated August 28, 2010.

4. One wonders what part of the Russian Federation the North Atlantic Treaty Organization (NATO) has war plans to invade.

5. The Barney Frank Sustainable Defense Task Force, July 2010, or what I term the "Sing Kubaya" Option.

6. This report was submitted to Congress on May 13, 2010, pursuant to Section 1251 of the National Defense Authorization Act for Fiscal Year 2010 (Public Law 111-84) and thus is known as the "1251 Report."

7. James Acton and Michael Gerson, "Beyond New Start," *Arms Control Today*, September 2011: "Russia is increasingly concerned with U.S. conventional capability, long range prompt conventional strike, weaponization of space, our upload capability on our strategic forces and ballistic missile capability" and thus is "reluctant to engage in further arms control." Russian Duma members have told me in private conversations they wish to curtail exactly those four areas of development. These concerns are then used by U.S. analysts as "proof" that such U.S. restraint will bring about the new agreements we seek.

8. Gerson and Acton say U.S. restraint on development has led to Russian cooperation on United Nations sanctions on Iran and "may help garner greater international support for nonproliferation initiatives. . . ."

9. *Geopolitics and Crisis in the Caucasus: From Chyzmyz*, January 20, 2010:

> Although military confrontation between Russia and the Western great powers in the Caucasus is unlikely, current power projection by both sides will create an unstable situation in the region, threatening peace and security in one of the mostly volatile regions of the contemporary world. Indeed, one point is certain: Russia will no longer tolerate any security arrangements between the Caucasian states and the outside powers as it sees such arrangements as an encroachment of its immediate security environment.

ABOUT THE CONTRIBUTORS

STEPHEN J. BLANK has served as the Strategic Studies Institute's authority on the Soviet bloc and the post-Soviet world since 1989. Prior to that he was Associate Professor of Soviet Studies at the Center for Aerospace Doctrine, Research, and Education, Maxwell Air Force Base, Alabama, and taught at the University of Texas, San Antonio, and the University of California, Riverside. Dr. Blank is the editor of *Imperial Decline: Russia's Changing Position in Asia*, coeditor of *Soviet Military and the Future*, and author of *The Sorcerer as Apprentice: Stalin's Commissariat of Nationalities, 1917-1924*. He has also written many articles and conference papers on Russia, the Commonwealth of Independent States, and Eastern European security issues. Dr. Blank's current research deals with proliferation and the revolution in military affairs, and energy and security in Eurasia. His two most recent books are *Russo-Chinese Energy Relations: Politics in Command*, London, UK: Global Markets Briefing, 2006; and *Natural Allies? Regional Security in Asia and Prospects for Indo-American Strategic Cooperation*, Carlisle, PA: Strategic Studies Institute, U.S. Army War College, 2005. Dr. Blank holds a B.A. in history from the University of Pennsylvania, and an M.A. and Ph.D. in history from the University of Chicago.

PETER R. HUESSY is President of Geostrategic Analysis, and Senior Fellow in National Security at the American Foreign Policy Council, and Senior Defense Consultant to the Air Force Association.

JACOB W. KIPP currently is an Adjunct Professor at the University of Kansas and a weekly columnist on Eurasian Security of the Jamestown Foundations. He served for many years at the Foreign Military Studies Office (FMSO) at Ft. Leavenworth, KS.

STEVEN PIFER (Ambassador, Ret.) is a Senior Fellow at the Brookings Center on the United States and Europe and Director of the Brookings Arms Control Initiative. He focuses on arms control, Russia, and Ukraine. He has offered commentary regarding Russia, Ukraine, and arms control issues on CNN, Fox News, National Public Radio, and Voice of America.